# LALIQUE GLASS

*Vase in blue glass with inlaid floral panels, circa 1912, wheel cut R. LALIQUE, height 11½ in. (30 cm.).*

# LALIQUE GLASS

## By Nicholas M. Dawes

C.1

CROWN PUBLISHERS, INC.   NEW YORK

To the memory of my father

Copyright © 1986 by Nicholas M. Dawes

Published by Crown Publishers, Inc., 225 Park Avenue South, New York,
New York 10003, and simultaneously in Canada by
General Publishing Company Limited

CROWN is a trademark of Crown Publishers, Inc.
Manufactured in Japan

Library of Congress Cataloging-in-Publication Data

Dawes, Nicholas M.
  Lalique glass.

  Bibliography: p.
  Includes index.
  1. Lalique, René, 1860–1945.   2. René Lalique et cie.
3. Glassware—France—History—19th century.
4. Glassware—France—History—20th century.
I. Title.
NK5198.L44D39  1986     748.294     85-9672
ISBN 0-517-55835-1

Design by Alan Benjamin

10  9  8  7  6  5  4  3  2  1
First Edition

PHOTOGRAPH CREDITS
*Photographs by Terry McGinniss, New York City:*
Figures 1, 4, 9, 11, 12, 15, 17, 18, 19, 20, 21, 22, 25, 27, 30, 32, 33,
34, 35, 39, 45, 46, 47, 48, 49, 50, 53, 56, 59, 60, 62, 63, 64, 67, 68, 69,
71, 72, 73, 74, 78, 79, 80, 81, 82, 83, 84, 86, 87, 88, 89, 90, 91, 92, 93,
94, 95, 96, 97, 98, 99, 100, 102, 104, 105, 110, 114, 115, 116, 118,
119, 122, 123, 125, 128, 129, 131, 132, 136, 138, 139, 142, 143, 145,
146, 147, 150, 151, 155, 159, 162, 163, 165, 166, 167, 171, 172, 173,
175, 176, 177, 178, 179, 180, 182, 184, 188, 189, 190, 191, 192, 194,
195, 200, 201, 202, 203, 204, 207, 208, 209, 211, 212, 213, 214, 215,
216, 217, 218, 219, 220, 221, 222, 228, 230, 231, 232, 233, 234, 235,
237, 240, 242, 250, 251, 252, 254, 255, 257, 260, 261.

*Photographs by Tim Benko, Benko Photography, Boulder, Colorado:*
Figures 16, 23, 31, 36, 37, 40, 41, 42, 43, 51, 52, 66, 76, 101, 103,
108, 112, 117, 120, 121, 124, 127, 130, 133, 134, 135, 137, 140, 141,
144, 148, 153, 154, 156, 158, 160, 161, 168, 169, 170, 181, 183, 196,
197, 205, 223, 226, 229, 253, 256, 258.

*Photographs by permission of Roger J. and Marion L. Mouré:*
*(Photographed by Terry McGinniss)*
Figures 38, 45, 59, 77, 78, 93, 100, 110, 111, 115, 119, 129, 136, 171,
172, 173, 175, 204, 213, 235, 240, 242.

# CONTENTS

# ACKNOWLEDGMENTS

Of all the individuals who have contributed to the preparation of *Lalique Glass*, I would like to begin by thanking my wife, Rosemarie, for her faithful support, financially and emotionally, of the project. Second, I wish to thank Terry McGinniss, who is responsible for the majority of the photography work used in the book, and Tim Benko, who also supplied excellent photographs from his studio in Colorado. I am indebted to Roger J. and Marion L. Mouré for allowing me to publish photographs of Lalique glass formerly in their collection (a full list of photograph credits appears on the copyright page).

I wish to thank every Lalique collector and enthusiast who has helped in the preparation, especially David and Lynn Weinstein, Mr. and Mrs. V. James Cole, and the muralist Abraham Joel Tobias, all of whom allowed me to photograph and record their collections. I am indebted to the following auction houses that supplied me with illustrative material: Phillips, Christie's, and Sotheby's in New York, and Bonhams in London. I also acknowledge the numerous galleries and dealers who have shared their knowledge, inventory, and reference material with me, especially Gallerie Moderne in London and Renee Antiques in New York.

I would like to thank the Museum Department of the Calouste Gulbenkian Foundation in Lisbon, and the staff of the Corning Museum of Glass in Corning, New York. I gratefully acknowledge the cooperation I have received from the Lalique Company, and would like to mention Lloyd Glasgow and Paul Lerner of Jacques Jugeat, Inc., New York, who supplied me with much of the information and illustrations of Cristal Lalique products used in Chapter 6 of this book.

I extend a special thanks to Laurens and Lorraine Tartasky, owners of Crystal Galleries of Boulder, Colorado, who welcomed me to their home, their library, and their remarkable Lalique collection during my period of research, and provided much of the valuable reference and illustrative material for *Lalique Glass*.

Lalique's glass has the ethereal brilliance of Arctic ice. Its texture is hardly visible, and one can scarcely believe that it was once a thick, opaque substance . . . ; it would seem rather to consist of immaterial ether, the frozen breath of the Polar night.

Guillaume Janneau,
*Modern Glass*, 1931

# LALIQUE GLASS

# 1. THE JEWELER WHO DISCOVERED GLASS (1860–1905)

Few individual designers have been able to achieve the level of artistic output, diversity, and influence enjoyed by René Lalique in his long and prosperous lifetime. By the time of his death, in 1945, Lalique had forged two careers and become master of both—the first, as a designer of exquisite jewelry, was ended before World War I, when he turned to his second career of glassmaking, a pursuit in which the Lalique Company earned a reputation for excellence which continues to the present day.

René Jules Lalique was born on April 6, 1860, in the village of Ay, located in the *département* of Marne in the former Champagne province of France. In 1862 the family moved to suburban Paris, where Lalique pursued his early education at the Lycée Turgot near Vincennes. The untimely death of his father, in 1876, forced Lalique to seek full-time employment, and at the age of sixteen he became apprenticed to the jeweler and goldsmith Louis Aucoc. Aucoc was among the leading de luxe jewelers in Paris, working in the fashionable neobaroque style and making extensive use of the wealth of diamonds and other gemstones that flooded into fashionable Europe from the recently opened African mines. The young apprentice probably gained practical experience under Aucoc, learning rudimentary skills and the properties of a jeweler's raw materials.

In 1878 René Lalique journeyed to London to further his education and settled among the French immigrant community in Sydenham, where he studied at the College de Sydenham, according to Henri Vever,[1] who chronicled the events some thirty years

Figure 1. Portrait of René Lalique, about thirty years of age.

later. The "college" Vever refers to was probably the School of Art which had been established in the Crystal Palace, built in 1851 and reerected in Sydenham in 1854. The college enjoyed limited success and closed in 1880, the year Lalique returned to France. It is unclear why he ventured outside his native country at the age of eighteen. He may have been taking advantage of a scholarship offered by his employer or by the School of Art or, more likely, he was drawn to England by the blossoming arts and crafts movement, whose ideals and concepts were refreshingly distinct from those of fashionable Paris society and clearly more sympathetic to his own. At Sydenham Lalique turned his attention to graphic design, combining the love of flora and fauna he had nurtured since childhood with his own developing sense of esthetics to conceive the unique, naturalistic style which was to become his trademark as a *joaillier*.

Lalique returned to France amid a reawakening of interest there in the decorative arts and crafts—a reaction against the smothering influence on artistic initiative which was perceived as a product of the machine age. Under the promotional guidance of numerous societies and organizations the movement gained momentum after the opening of the Musée des Arts Décoratifs in 1882 and the doors of Paris salons began to open to *les arts mineurs*. René Lalique rode the crest of this wave of artistic enthusiasm for the remainder of the nineteenth century, emerging by 1900 as one of its leading influential figures.

In Paris Lalique found employment for his graphic talents by designing wallpaper and fabrics for a relative, M. Vuilleret, and completed his education with a course of study in sculpture and modeling techniques under Justin Lequien at the Ecole Bernard Palissy.

Lalique's studies under Lequien were an important part of the process of acquiring necessary skills for the establishment of a diversified atelier, and reflected his desire to execute work on a larger scale.

By 1881, with the assistance of a friend, Varenne, Lalique began to work as a freelance jewelry designer, assembling an impressive list of patrons that included Cartier, Boucheron, Hamelin, and Jules Destape. In the winter of 1885 Lalique purchased a small workshop on the Place Gaillon from Jules Destape, who subsequently retired to Algeria.[2] He began operations early in 1886 with a small work force, partly inherited from Destape, including a foreman named Briançon and perhaps a dozen others. Lalique was able to concentrate on the innovative jewelry for which he was becoming known, respected, and increasingly patronized, publishing his designs regularly in the trade journal *Le Bijou*, where they drew admiration from Alphonse Fouquet and his son Georges. Working in his own interpretation of the emerging Art Nouveau style, which inspired Georges Fouquet's *mille neuf cent* style, Lalique made increasing use of novel and inexpensive materials in his creations, including translucent enamels, semiprecious stones, ivory, and hard stones (Figure 2).

René Lalique rapidly outgrew his first atelier and, in 1887, rented a second location on the Rue du Quatre Septembre. The two workshops probably operated simultaneously until 1890, when Lalique acquired new premises at 20 Rue Thérèse, which included enough space for his work force of thirty people.[3] In the same year, Lalique married the daughter of the sculptor Auguste Ledru, and the couple settled in a third-floor apartment above the Rue Thérèse atelier. It was in this workshop that Lalique created his celebrated commissions for the actress Sarah Bernhardt, and the magnificent Art Nouveau jewelry and *objects vertu* which earned him the patronage and admiration of Samuel Bing, the German art dealer who opened his Paris shop, La Maison de l'Art Nouveau, in 1895 (Figure 3).

*Figure 2. Hair comb in horn, enamel, and diamonds, Circa 1895, height 6½ in. (16 cm.).*

René Lalique consistently sought out new materials for use in jewelry, a search that led to his discovery of glass. He was the first *joaillier* to work in horn, sculpting it naturalistically to a daring degree. *Calouste Gulbenkian Museum, Lisbon*

*Figure 3. Diadem in gold, horn, translucent enamels, and single amethyst, circa 1900, height 3½ in. (9 cm.).*

Lalique's jewelry became increasingly bizarre and flamboyant by the turn of the century. Many of his more outrageous creations were commissioned by patrons in the theatrical profession, including Sarah Bernhardt. The amethyst is a replacement for the original, paler stone. *Calouste Gulbenkian Museum, Lisbon*

It was also at the Rue Thérèse premises that René Lalique began to experiment with properties of glass. He was persistently exploring the potential of new materials for use in jewelry, and the choice of glass was a predictable development from his extensive use of vitreous enamels at that time. Figure 4 illustrates a core-molded perfume vial and stopper cast in glass in the *cire perdue*, or "lost wax," technique, which, simply defined, requires the carving of a master model out of wax; the model is used to make a vitreous mold from which duplicates of the wax master can be cast in glass or metal.[4] The vial, which was made during René Lalique's earliest period of experimentation with glass, remained among his personal possessions un-

4

*Figure 4. Glass perfume vial and stopper made in the* cire perdue *technique, length 4 in. (10 cm.).*

This may be the earliest all-glass object by Lalique, made in his Rue Thérèse workshop around 1893. *Phillips, New York*

til his death and was on loan to the Musée du Louvre from 1925. An account of its manufacture was included in a brochure of an exhibition in New York in 1935, in which the vial was featured:

> In [Lalique's] own kitchen he made his first experiment with pure glass. . . . a tiny tear bottle, a droplike gem, molded in a simple cooking pan over the fire in his stove in the Rue Thérèse. He piled on the wood, hotter grew the flame. . . . In the intense heat Lalique

worked, alone, oblivious to his surroundings. Suddenly he became aware of cracking timbers; his studio was afire, his experiment in danger. While his landlord rushed to put out the fire, Lalique saved his original experiment in glass.[5]

Although this account is clearly fanciful, it is embroidered rather than concocted and it is quite probable that the vial is the earliest surviving example of Lalique glass. It was most likely made as part of a batch in the atelier, which was equipped with a small kiln or furnace of the type used in enameling. Lalique's period of experimentation with all-glass objects appears to have been short-lived and exceptional (literally a "flash in the pan" if we are to believe the above account), although he did not abandon the material altogether. The precise date of manufacture of the vial is not known, though it was probaby around 1893. By that time, Lalique was incorporating glass into his jewelry in the form of cast *pâte-de-verre* shapes in opaque colors and shallow-relief plaques in clear, colored, or opalescent glass (Figure 5).

The design and manufacture of these early plaques may have been influenced by the pioneering work of Henri Cros (1840–1907), who developed a technique for casting glass in the form of *pâte-de-verre* in the 1890s. Cros drew his inspiration from Greek and Roman medallions in glass paste, which were first exhibited in Paris in 1878, and Lalique adopted the classical designs preferred by Cros for his own figural style.

Although the perfume vial is the only recorded example, Vever[6] describes several other pieces that resulted from Lalique's earliest experiments with glass between 1891 and 1894, including a "head of John the Baptist," a goblet, and "panels molded with mythological figures in relief." It can be assumed that these objects were cast in the *cire perdue* technique, which was rarely used in glassmaking in the 1890s but was a common and universal method of bronze casting which Lalique practiced.

During his residence at the Rue Thérèse premises, René Lalique made increasing use of bronze, designing and casting small sculptures and plaques and using the metal in combination with other materials for his *objets vertu*. Lalique's decision to work in bronze was probably encouraged by his father-in-law, Auguste Ledru, and brother-in-law of the same name, who were both sculptors, and it is likely that Lalique was introduced to the *cire perdue* process through its application in decorative bronze work and probably

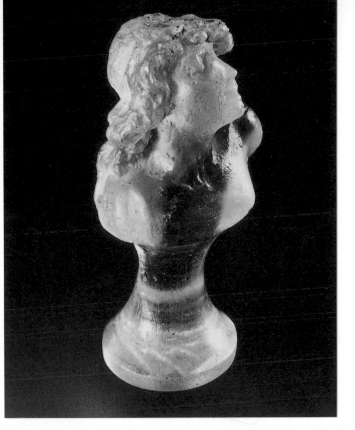

*Figure 6. Figural seal in* cire perdue *glass, circa 1895–1900, molded* LALIQUE, *height 2 in. (5.2 cm.).*

The similarities between this tiny object and the popular bronze seals made contemporaneously suggest that Lalique may have learned the *cire perdue* technique from its applications in decorative bronze work. *Collection of Charles and Mary Magriel*

*Figure 5. Silver and glass pendant in the Art Nouveau taste, circa 1898, height 3¼ in. (8.3 cm.).*

Lalique began incorporating glass into his jewelry in the mid-1890s; this example features a "mask" cast in opalescent glass which may have been duplicated and used in a number of similar designs. The pendant baroque pearl is a characteristic feature. *Calouste Gulbenkian Museum, Lisbon*

by his wife's family. The sculptural nature of his early creations as described by Vever lend support to this theory, further strengthened by the seal illustrated in Figure 6. The seal, which is engraved with an unidentified "AB" monogram, closely resembles bronze examples of the mid-1890s in style and scale, and was probably cast at Rue Thérèse before 1900. The "panels" mentioned by Vever may also have been cast as the direct result of the experiences in bronze shared by Lalique and his family, including the casting of a

6 portrait plaque of his bride in *cire perdue* bronze in the early 1890s.[7]

By the late 1890s Lalique was casting larger panels in glass and began to exhibit bas-reliefs in translucent glass. Figure 7 illustrates a decorative plaque in frosted glass which may date from that time, when

Figure 7. Frosted glass plaque with intaglio molded decoration, circa 1900, overall dimensions 18 in. × 16½ in. (45.7 cm. × 42 cm.).

This unusual object, with heavenly host design, was probably made for a special commission. The contemporary bronze frame is stylistically similar to examples made in the late 1890s, at which time Lalique was exhibiting bas-reliefs in glass. © 1984 Sotheby Parke Bernet, Inc.

Lalique was technically equipped to manufacture it. The intaglio is characteristic of the shallow relief work favored by Lalique on contemporary jewelry and *objets* in ivory, alabaster, and metals, and the bronze frame is stylistically similar to cadres manufactured at Rue Thérèse around 1900. The panel was probably cast in a metal mold, unlike the *cire perdue* work, which was cast in ceramic molds.

Lalique's experiments with molded and sculptural glass may have been inspired and aided by the work of the sculptor Ringel D'Illzach, who experimented with the chemical properties of glass and the application of mechanical molding processes in the 1890s. The results and implications of Ringel's work were described by Jules Henrivaux in 1911:

> Chemistry, combined with mechanization, allows glass to be molded in a wide variety of ways, as evidenced in the work of the sculptor Ringel [who] showed several curious pieces of glass at the salon of 1898, plaques and medallions executed in a most unusual manner. If his process were to be used in combination with sophisticated mechanical techniques, we would be able to cast glass in any hollow mold, duplicating any form, including sculpture, and one can imagine the revolutionary impact on industry! Glass would become an artist's most collaborative material and could be substituted for bronze, marble, or terra-cotta to suit the taste of the sculptor. . . . There are elements in architecture which would benefit immediately from this transformation, from a decorative view and for important sanitary reasons.[8]

René Lalique recognized the commercial potential in the malleable properties of Ringel's glass and developed his own glass body, termed *demi-cristal*, with the same properties.

From the late 1890s Lalique manufactured an increasing number of small, decorative objects using glass in combination with other materials, mostly bronze, silver, alabaster, ivory, and copper foil (Figure 8). To achieve these incongruous combinations Lalique drew upon his experience as a jeweler and enameler and conducted a series of experiments in the control of temperature and application of heat to the various materials during assembly.[9] Although by 1900 he employed several dozen craftsmen he carried out much of the critical work himself, as he did throughout much of his career. Lalique's personal contributions to his craft were recorded in the magazine *Art et Décoration* in 1902:

> In the realization of his work René Lalique is possessed with the singular habits of a practitioner. He is not content with drawing designs on paper, he has to execute them himself. Therefore, he must function as a sculptor, enameler, goldsmith, and painter, and he does all of this in excellent fashion. Consider the work involved in glass figurines: he must cut and mold the glass and then apply the hand of a watercolorist. He has used every skill in the modeler's repertoire in his work.[10]

Although Lalique was casting glass into molds by 1902, hollow objects were free-blown, usually directly into metal armatures, including a few unique objects made before 1900 and exhibited at the Paris Exposi-

*Figure 8. Chalice in copper and blown glass, with figural knop in cire perdue glass, circa 1903–1904, height 8½ in. (21 cm.).*

Many of Lalique's early designs in glass were of chalice or goblet form. Items of this type were frequently exhibited to impress and tempt discriminating patrons. This example was exhibited at Agnew's Gallery in London in 1905 and acquired by Calouste Gulbenkian in 1910 following its display at the Musée Galliera in Paris. *Calouste Gulbenkian Museum, Lisbon*

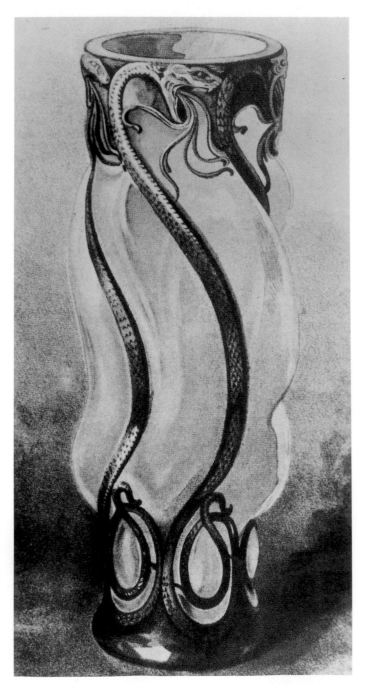

tion Universelle of that year (Figure 9). The exhibition attracted over 50 million visitors in six months and René Lalique's sensational contribution of jewelry, ivory and bronze work, and elaborate *objets vertu* confirmed his position as *chef d'école* of French decorative art, a reputation already established among his contemporaries, including Emile Gallé, who had called him "the supreme exponent of the *Beaux Arts*."[11]

Despite his constant exploration of new materials, Lalique achieved a consistency in quality and style by designing everything himself. Even though he employed talented artists, among them the American sculptor Gaston Lachaise, who worked for Lalique for a brief period in 1905,[12] and the jeweler Eugène Feuillâtre, the pupil of Alphonse Mucha and Georges Fouquet, there is no evidence that their own designs were executed. Lalique's design policy was not shared by his glassmaking contemporaries, preeminent among whom were Louis Comfort Tiffany in the United States and Emile Gallé in France, both of whom employed highly skilled designers as well as craftsmen. Gallé's unique masterpieces relied for their success on the florid, organic forms of the Art Nouveau style, a splendid use of color, and a combination of immense technical skill, patience, artistry, and serendipity. As part of his display at the 1900 Exposition, Gallé erected a mock glass kiln around which were strewn hundreds of shards and "wasters."

*Figure 9. Vase in opalescent glass blown into a metal armature, circa 1898.*

This vase was one of a small number of glass items included in Lalique's display at the 1900 Exposition. Lalique practiced the technique of blowing glass into a metal armature from the 1890s until about 1905, when he developed the process of mold-blowing. *Reprinted from* Art et Décoration, *December 1898.*

The objective of this "sacrificial altar" was to impress upon the public the high incidence of wastage in Gallé's craft and to emphasize the importance of the perfect examples.

It is likely that René Lalique saw this display as a warning rather than as a sacred icon and, despite the predominant approval for handcraftsmanship at the turn of the century, Lalique chose not to pursue studio production and steered a different course from Gallé at the beginning of his glassmaking career. He did not reject or react against the popular styles, he simply introduced his own taste and innovations into decorative glass, seeking to control the properties of the material, to exploit its best quality—translucence—and to eliminate haphazardness in design and manufacture. Random, organic forms were contrary to this approach, as were mottled colors, however harmonious the result.

In 1902 Lalique continued his experiments with casting glass reliefs at a family estate in the picturesque village of Clairfontaine, about twenty-four miles southwest of Paris, with a staff of four, which probably consisted of a foreman, or *chef de place*, two *ceuilleurs*, who supervised the melting and pouring of glass, and a *gamin*, or boy helper.[13] Glass was made at Clairfontaine for at least ten years. It is unclear how much time Lalique spent at Clairfontaine and what facilities were available there, though Gustave Kahn notes: "[At Clairfontaine] Lalique worked in rudimentary conditions, much more basic than those of larger glassworks."[14]

Glass was made at the estate from raw materials, whereas in the Paris workshops it was purchased in the form of vitreous blocks, and the site was probably used for the manufacture of larger objects in glass and for experimentation. Lalique increased the scale of his molds and began to manufacture glass for interior and exterior architectural designs. The use of glass as an element in architecture was not an entirely new idea in France at the time and Lalique was able to view displays of glass *dallages*, or paving slabs, at the 1900 Exposition which had been used for the floors and staircases of several Paris bank buildings and railroad stations in the nineteenth century, including the Gare Quai d'Orsay. This *pierre de verre* was in the form of heavy, square slabs, produced in France and the United States by manufacturers of flat glass, windows, etc. René Lalique was the first artist to adopt the idea and to design decorative panels, the earliest of which were cast at Clairfontaine, probably in 1902.

In that year, Lalique collaborated with an architect named Feine[15] on the renovation of a building to incorporate workshops, an exhibition area, and accommodations. The result was an impressive structure with neo-Gothic façade at 40 Cours la Reine (now called Cours Albert 1er), near the Place de la Concorde on the Right Bank of the Seine in Paris, work on which was completed in December 1902.[16] Lalique's *hôtel* on the Cours la Reine consisted of five stories, the ground and first floors functioning as an exhibition gallery and retail outlet which allowed Lalique to present and market his works through his own address (Figure 14). The metal entrance doors were glazed with unique frosted glass panels cast with pine branches in shallow relief (Figure 10), a superb technical and artistic achievement that can still be admired today and which prompted scores of architectural commissions around the globe for the next forty years.

The expanded workshop premises allowed increased production to meet the demands created by Lalique's success at the 1900 Exposition. Though the emphasis was still on jewelry production, new "Laliques" were introduced to tempt his established and discriminating clientele, among whom were some of the wealthiest and most powerful individuals in Europe. Products included an increasing number of *objets vertu*: paper knives, boxes, statuettes, and vessels in glass and metal (Figures 11 and 13), the majority of

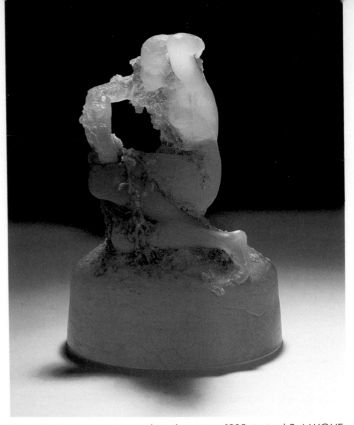

*Figure 10. The glass doors of Lalique's Paris atelier, installed in 1902.*

René Lalique was the first glassmaker of the 20th century to adopt the technique of casting glass blocks for decorative use.

*Figure 11. Figurine in* cire perdue *glass, circa 1905, incised R. LALIQUE, height 5 in. (12.5 cm.).*

Figurines and statuettes were among Lalique's earliest all-glass creations, cast from wax *maquettes* which were almost certainly modeled by René Lalique. The use of sepia-colored *patine* to highlight the relief is characteristic. *Weinstein Collection*

which were designed and assembled as unique objects, although Lalique gradually introduced duplicated elements, as he had in jewelry designs of a few years earlier (Figure 5).

Within the first few years of residence at Cours la Reine, Lalique began to manufacture objects in series, the earliest of which, closely resembling the unique objects produced contemporaneously, included the chalice in silver and free-blown opalescent

its handsome proportions, the chalice displays the first step toward simplification of line in Lalique's design (in comparison to the vessels in Figures 8 and 13, for example), a function of the techniques employed in its manufacture. Although the chalice was made before Lalique had begun to blow glass into molds, probably in 1904, it can be considered the earliest of his mass-produced glass vessels, an innocent yet triumphant herald of the glorious glassmaking career which lay ahead.

*Figure 12. Chalice in opalescent glass and silver, circa 1904, stamped R. LALIQUE 32 on foot rim, height 8 in. (20 cm.).*

This chalice, made before Lalique had begun to blow glass into molds, is evidence of his earliest movement toward "mass production." The control number on the foot rim indicates that this example is number 32 in a series, from which at least five other identical models are known.

*Figure 13. "Sugar Bowl" and cover in opaque-green glass blown into a silver armature, circa 1903, height 8½ in. (22 cm.).*

The writhing serpent motif, a favorite of Lalique's, was never executed more dramatically than in this unique vessel. *Calouste Gulbenkian Museum, Lisbon*

glass illustrated in Figure 12. The control number stamped on the foot of this vessel indicates that it is number 32 in a series, at least five other examples of which are known, all with lower control numbers.

The chalice, which may have been accompanied originally by a paten, is decorated with the same pine branches which adorn the glass doors of Lalique's *hôtel* (Figure 10), and modeled in the Celtic-inspired style of the English arts and crafts movement. Despite

Figure 14. The Exhibition Gallery at 40 Cours la Reine, circa 1905.

Lalique designed this floor and mezzanine and was resident above it from 1902 until his death in 1945. The chandeliers are in blown opalescent glass; the "Serpent" mirror on the right is one of two exhibited at the 1900 Exposition, one of which is now in the Calouste Gulbenkian Museum, together with the centerpiece shown in the foreground. *Reprinted from L'Art Décoratif, May 1905. Photo: The Corning Museum of Glass, Corning, New York.*

# 2. THE DAWN OF AN EMPIRE (1905–1915)

Paris was a culturally divided city at the turn of the century: Brimming with the esthetic fantasies and vaudeville atmosphere of La Belle Epoque, the city was also experiencing Fin de Siècle pessimism, evidenced in the taste for neoclassicism and the neo-Romanesque and glorified in the numerous retrospective displays at the 1900 Exposition.

The influences of the former movement were to dominate the first years of the twentieth century. As modern art was being nurtured in gallery exhibitions of Fauvist and Cubist painting, a desire arose among artists and art critics alike to cultivate and improve the decorative arts by combining the talents of French designers with the technology of the machine age, and to discourage the manufacture of exclusive, unimaginative *objets* favored by a wealthy clientele.

It was in this climate of optimism that René Lalique opened his first Paris retail premises, in 1905, located at 24 Place Vendôme. In the same year Samuel Bing died and René Lalique, aged forty-five, inherited the role and influence of his former patron, a position he was to maintain for another thirty years.

For his debut exhibition at the Place Vendôme Lalique designed an invitation in the form of an Art Nouveau bronze medallion (Figure 15). Bronze was among Lalique's favorite materials in 1905 (in previous years he had fashioned exhibition announcements in ivory), and it was not until seven years later that Lalique issued a glass medallion as an invitation

*Figure 15. Bronze medallion cast in the cire perdue technique, 1905, signed with initials R.L., diameter 2½ in. (6.5 cm.).*

The successful combination of Art Nouveau and neoclassicism in this design is typical of Lalique's style in 1905. The signature confirms that the *maquette* for this medallion was sculpted in wax by René Lalique. *Phillips, New York*

(Figure 36). Within a few years of operations at the Place Vendôme, however, René Lalique was recognized as the unofficial *maître verrier* of France, the worthy successor to Emile Gallé, who had died in 1904.

Among the great French entrepreneurial visionaries of the early twentieth century was a young Corsican named François Coty, who had developed an interest in perfumes in the 1890s and founded the House of Coty in 1904. At that time French perfume was a relatively inexpensive commodity, high in quality but lacking the variety and prestige associated with name brands and manufacturers. It was common for individual druggists to concoct their own scents and eau de colognes, offering them for sale in plain glass pharmaceutical bottles wrapped in waxed paper. Success came rapidly to François Coty, largely due to the popularity of his La Rose Jacqueminot perfume, and he soon established retail premises on the fashionable Place Vendôme adjacent to René Lalique's newly opened showroom. This proximity gave Coty the opportunity to admire Lalique's designs, mostly limited at that time to jewelry and *objets vertu*, and, in 1907, he commissioned Lalique to design labels, and subsequently bottles and flasks, for his expanding range of fragrances, which included traditional floral perfumes and newly introduced products of a chemical base. René Lalique applied his skills as a jeweler and goldsmith to the labels he designed for Coty in metal and card (Figure 16). He was not unfamiliar with perfume

*Figure 16. A selection of Coty perfume bottles including a tester box, circa 1907–1910.*

The gilt-metal bas relief plaque on the tester box was designed by René Lalique and signed by him. The plain form of the bottles is typical of the earliest commissions from Coty, which were manufactured at the Legras and Company glassworks. *Crystal Galleries*

*Figure 17. Flask and stopper in clear and frosted glass, circa 1905–1912, wheel-cut R. LALIQUE, height 10 in. (25.5 cm.).*

Bottles and flasks in blown glass were probably on sale at Lalique's Place Vendôme premises at the time of his meeting with François Coty in 1907. *Phillips, New York*

bottle manufacture, having made his first attempt at the Rue Thérèse atelier (Figure 4), and had begun to blow glass into molds before 1905.[1]

It is probable that decorative bottles and flasks, together with drinking glasses, were on sale at the Place Vendôme by the time of Lalique's meeting with Coty in 1907 (Figure 17), when Lalique exhibited a number of thin-walled vessels of mold-blown manufacture.[2] Lalique's glassmaking career was still in its infancy, however, and he was not technically equipped to meet the demands of large-scale production which Coty needed. For this reason, Lalique's earliest commissions from Coty were manufactured at the glassworks of Legras and Company of St. Denis, a large, established concern of close to 1,500 employees. The bottles manufactured at Legras were, in the author's opinion, limited to the plain-bodied square or rectangular type with decorative stoppers and labels designed by Lalique. The Legras bottles have several

*Figure 18. Two perfume bottles for Coty fragrances, circa 1909, height of taller 4½ in. (11.4 cm.).*

These two bottles are from a boxed set of six containing François Coty's earliest commercial fragrances: Ambre Antique, L'Aimant, La Rose Jacqueminot, Chypre, Styx, and Origan. The Ambre Antique bottle in this photograph was made at Lalique's Combs-la-Ville Glassworks, probably in 1909, and is signed Lalique. Note the "warmer" quality of the glass and softer edges in comparison to the L'Aimant bottle, which was made at the Legras works and is unsigned.

*Figure 19. Signature on the Ambre Antique bottle in Figure 18. This signature type is referred to as the "extended L."*

features that distinguish them from the earliest products of Lalique's own glassworks (Figure 18). First, they do not bear an impressed signature, although the word COTY is sometimes present; second, the glass is clearer and brighter; and third, the glass is crisply molded and sharper-edged to the touch. The two latter characteristics are evidence that Legras used glass of a higher lead content than that of the *demi-cristal* favored by Lalique. From his earliest work in glass René Lalique used a potash glass body with a lead oxide content of around 12 percent, one-half of the lead content required for the glass to be labeled *cristal* under French statutes. Termed *demi-cristal*, Lalique's glass was well suited to mold blowing and mass production, being relatively inexpensive, highly malleable in its semimolten state, unlikely to adhere to the mold during cooling, and requiring little surface treatment on removal from a mold.

In the early part of 1909 Lalique rented his first glassworks, located at Combs-la-Ville, about thirty-six miles east of Paris, near Fontainebleau. The area's unique geology included the *sables de Fontainebleau*, sands famous for their extraordinarily high silica content, which had attracted glassmakers to the region for centuries. Lalique probably employed between fifty and one hundred people initially at Combs-la-Ville, chiefly in the manufacture of commercial perfume bottles. The technology required for mass production was partly borrowed from the French wine and pharmaceutical bottle industries, including the

molding techniques developed by Claude Boucher at his wine bottle and flacon manufactory in Cognac. Boucher pioneered the revolving mold and *moule de bague* (ring mold), which included male and female parts, as well as improving methods of introducing glass into molds, taking out a total of thirteen patents on his devices between 1894 and 1903.[3]

The most important development stemming from this technology was the introduction of precision-cast metal molds for decorative glass manufacture. Metal was rarely used before the advent of large-scale production owing to its high cost compared to vitreous materials or wood. The enormous variety of Lalique's perfume bottle designs required sophisticated, semi-automated processes of manufacture. Depending on the form of the vessel, the technique employed was either *pressé soufflé*—where the glass was blown into a hinged double mold, by either mouth or bellows—or *aspiré soufflé*—which entailed sucking the "gather" of glass into a mold automatically by creating a vacuum within it. Flacons of simpler design, and those made in larger quantities in later years, were all made automatically. No free-blown examples are recorded.

The success of his commercial designs allowed René Lalique to purchase the Combs-la-Ville Glassworks in 1910, by which time he had already begun to manufacture decorative bottles, flacons, and powder boxes for his retail premises. The bottles were sold without contents on the assumption that perfume from plain containers could be decanted into them for use at the dressing table (Figures 22 and 23). The idea of a reusable glass perfume bottle was not new, but Lalique's molded flacons were the first affordable examples made to attract a mass market yet with the quality to lure an elegant élite.

*Figure 20. Perfume bottle with "tiara" stopper for Leurs Ames fragrance by D'Orsay, circa 1914, molded Lalique with "extended L," height 5 in. (13 cm.). Phillips, New York*

The earliest of these bottles were in clear glass, of flattened form, molded in shallow or intaglio relief in the manner Lalique favored as jeweler, and often highlighted with blue, gray, or sepia *patine* (Figure 21). *Patine* was a form of enamel which Lalique employed to stain or color recessed areas of decoration in glass. Stoppers were always solid glass and were cast separately, usually in molds of two half-sections. Each stopper was carefully fitted into the body with the aid of carborundum powder, a process known in France as *bouchon à l'émeri*, which gives the familiar granular, frosted appearance to neck and stopper and ensures tightness and retrievability. When fitted, stopper and bottle were engraved with corresponding control numbers, which appear on the majority of René Lalique's stoppered vessels, including commercial perfume bottles, and serve today as useful clues for detecting "marriages." Stoppers were occasionally designed to function as droppers, especially on larger eau de cologne bottles, but were normally a decorative element, always cleverly designed in harmony with the body of the vessel.

The commercial genius of François Coty and his followers (the founders of Lancôme, Orlane, and Charles of the Ritz were all his employees), combined with the design skills of René Lalique, led to an unprecedented expansion of the French perfume industry. The formula consisted of fine perfumes presented in attractive containers at equally attractive prices. Initially the greatest successes were in domestic consumption, but the market rapidly grew to international proportions. Between 1913 and 1920 the value of exports of perfume products from France increased from 60 million francs to 700 million francs,[4] much of it due to demand from the United States. The in-

17

*Figure 21. Perfume bottle with lizard decoration, circa 1912, engraved R. Lalique, height 4¼ in. (10.5 cm.). Weinstein Collection*

dustry earned a new respect and status. Attracted by commercial potential and artistic respectability, numerous fashion houses and couturiers began to manufacture and market perfumes. By the 1920s *parfumerie* was considered an admirable and respectable branch of the decorative arts.

The Combs-la-Ville Glassworks enabled René Lalique to concentrate on designing glass objects to meet the combined demands of an expanding clientele and his own creative fertility. In 1915, six years after it opened, the factory was forced to close soon after the outbreak of World War I. Some of René La-

lique's finest designs date from this first period of manufacture, during which he faced and overcame the challenges of a new material and new technology.

Among his earliest accomplishments was the design and manufacture of decorative vases, the first of which were made by the *cire perdue* process. While Lalique cannot be credited with inventing or even introducing *cire perdue* glass, he was the first artist of the twentieth century to employ the technique successfully in the making of blown-glass vessels, a process he practiced with repeated success until the late 1920s. Before 1904 Lalique had blown glass only in combination with other materials, mostly employing

*Figure 22. "4 Soleils" (Suns) perfume bottle, circa 1913, height 3 in. (7.5 cm.).*

Decorative bottles of this type held perfume, which was decanted from plainer containers for use at the dressing table. The four "suns" are cast-glass medallions set into the body of the vessel, radiating light, which is reflected by metal foil trapped inside the glass. *Collection of A. J. Tobias*

*Figure 23. Three Lalique perfume bottles, circa 1912–1923, including "Bouchon Mûres" (Mulberries) (center), height of tallest 4½ in. (11 cm.).*

The "tiara" stopper was a distinctive feature of Lalique's more expensive perfume bottles and examples in colored glass are extremely rare today. *Crystal Galleries*

Figure 24. Shade for a lighting fixture in cire perdue glass, circa 1909–1910, diameter 12½ in. (32 cm.).

The wax master mold for this remarkable design was almost certainly sculpted by René Lalique. *Calouste Gulbenkian Museum, Lisbon*

a metal armature (Figures 12 and 13), and his *cire perdue* work was limited to a few cast statuettes and plaques for use in jewelry.

It is uncertain whether the earliest *cire perdue* vessels were blown at the Combs-la-Ville Glassworks or at Clairfontaine, where Lalique was still making glass in 1912.[5] According to Gustave Kahn,[6] the output from Clairfontaine consisted mainly of molded panels of the type illustrated by Figure 10, and no mention is made of blown vessels in contemporary writings. It is probable that blowing apparatus did not exist at Clairfontaine and that the first hollow *cire perdue* vessels were made at Combs-la-Ville and thus date from 1909 or 1910.

The process for making a *cire perdue* vase differs from that for a statuette or plaque in that the former requires that the glass be blown into the mold, rather than poured or cast. In each case, preparation of the mold is the same: A master model or *maquette* is carved in wax and encased in a cast of semiplastic refractory clay. The clay hardens and the cast is warmed, melting the wax inside, which drains off through an aperture, leaving a hollow mold within the cast. Molten glass is introduced into the mold—poured if the object is to be solid, blown in the case of a hollow vessel—and allowed to cool and anneal, after which the mold is carefully destroyed and the object removed. The precise procedure that Lalique's craftsmen followed for the *cire perdue* work has never been revealed in detail, and examples of these remarkable *confidences d'artistes* always took pride of place whenever they were included in exhibitions.

R LALIQUE

The lamp shade illustrated in Figure 24, which was presumably intended to be hung from a ceiling fixture, may be one of the earliest blown-glass objects in *cire perdue* made at Combs-la-Ville. The glass is of the familiar semiopaque, frosted appearance, and the sumptuous design is highlighted with traces of sepia *patine*.

There is some evidence that René Lalique was responsible for modeling the unique *cire perdue* work himself, including numerous contemporary references to the designs as "personal." The "Lalique fingerprints," which are a feature of most *cire perdue* objects, are simply a serendipitous imprint of the modeler, however, not an intentional "signature." It is the author's belief that only a small proportion of the *maquettes* for *cire perdue* work were modeled by René Lalique, including the lamp shade in Figure 24. Other

*Figure 25. Hanging light bowl in cire perdue glass, circa 1910–1920, with original silk hanging cords, diameter 13¼ in. (33.5 cm.).*

The spreading "cracks," which are a surface feature of Lalique's *cire perdue* work, are caused by flaws in the ceramic mold which were penetrated by the molten glass upon introduction. These "feather marks" were only partially removed as they invariably transversed relief decoration. *Phillips, New York*

examples that can be attributed include those designs that are of a spontaneous or inspirational nature, or appear to have been modeled directly from natural specimens rather than to have been copied and interpreted by skilled modelers from sketched designs.

The hemispherical hanging shade illustrated in Figure 25 probably dates from 1912 to 1914 and may also have been modeled by René Lalique. Unlike the earlier shade in Figure 24, Lalique has exploited the translucent properties of the glass in this design of spreading *prunus* branches, which evidences the powerful influence of Japonisme.

Figure 26 illustrates what may be the earliest example of a blown *cire perdue* vase by René Lalique, probably made at the Combs-la-Ville Glassworks in 1909 or 1910. The form of the vessel is of secondary importance to its extraordinary decoration, consisting of four Medusan heads protruding at intervals from the body. The stylistic similarities between the Medusa heads and Lalique jewelry designs from about 1905 are apparent, and the use of heavy *patine* to highlight the design is characteristic of this period. The gro-

*Figure 27. Jar and cover of Oriental form in cire perdue glass, circa 1911–1913, wheel-cut R. LALIQUE, height 8 in. (20 cm.).*

The placement of the signatures on this vessel is characteristic of the 1910–1914 period. The *patine* was applied after the signature was added and has stained the lettering.

*Figure 28. Detail of the cover of Figure 27.*

*Figure 26. "Medusa" vase in cire perdue blown glass, circa 1909–1910, height 9 in. (23.5 cm.).*

The Medusa vase may be the earliest example of a Lalique *cire perdue* vase in blown glass. *Calouste Gulbenkian Museum, Lisbon*

tesque masks, which are in pink-tinted glass, were cast separately and applied after both elements had vitrified, a technique first used by Lalique in jewelry designs in the late 1890s (Figure 5), and rarely practiced in vase designs, though the effect was occasionally simulated in production models made by a single molding.

The Medusa vase was followed by a range of less ambitious *cire perdue* designs between 1910 and 1914, probably numbering a few dozen in total, which can be recognized by their style, signature type, and the absence of incised numerals which were added to *cire perdue* designs from 1919 (Figure 27).

22

*Figure 29. Box with hinged cover in black glass, circa 1913, wheel-cut R. LALIQUE, length 7½ in. (19 cm.).*

Some of Lalique's earliest designs made at the Combs-la-Ville Glassworks can be considered *objets vertu* in glass, intended to appeal to his established and highly discriminating clientele. The clasp and hinges of this exquisite box, one of four known to the author, are in silver-plated brass. *Christie's, New York*

René Lalique's *cire perdue* work has always been the most admired and the most highly valued of his creations—examples change hands today for five-figure sums—but *cire perdue* was considered an insignificant branch of production in Lalique's commercial empire. The unique objects were treated as exhibition pieces, offered for sale through select retail outlets and exhibitions, or made for special commission, and were never advertised in catalogues.

The most important move after the opening of the Combs-la-Ville Glassworks was toward mass production and duplication of designs, which were, typically, crisply outlined and highly polished, in contrast to the *cire perdue* work, which was rough, unpolished, and unsuitable for mass production or marketing.

In 1911 the Société des Artistes Décorateurs opened its salon at the Pavilion de Marsan with a display of glass in the "modern style," including designs by Maurice Dufrène, Paul Follot, and Léon Jallot. Described as "*un art fait de mesure, de logique, d'ordre et d'har-*

monie," [7] the style became the fashionable alternative to the Louis XVI revivalism favored by traditional interior designers, and set the precedent for a decade of decorative art.

In the same year, René Lalique began to manufacture glass in his own interpretation of the "modern style" and exhibited at the Pavilion de Marsan in 1912. Unlike the work of his contemporaries who sought to combine design and "Parisian taste" with studio production, Lalique's glass was blown, pressed, and cast in the manner of his perfume bottles and could be manufactured on an industrial scale. Lalique's approach met with immediate approval from the public and art critics alike, among them Nilsen Lauvrik, who wrote of Lalique's exhibition:

*Figure 30. Presentation chalice in clear and frosted glass, circa 1907–1912, stamped LALIQUE on gilt-metal mount, height 10½ in. (27 cm.).*

This unique vessel is engraved with an unidentified monogram and Latin motto, evidence that it was made for a special commission. *Weinstein Collection*

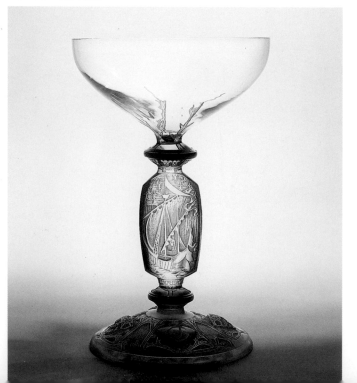

[René Lalique's] accomplished craftsmanship has enabled him to utilize the services of the machine without in the least affecting the artistic quality of his productions. In his hands, it is no longer mechanically meaningless; it has become a tool of the artist wherewith he may communicate his ideas to a greater number than was ever possible to the craftsmen of old.[8]

Lauvrik was perhaps the first of his generation to recognize this most important contribution to decorative art in the work of René Lalique.

Some of the products of the early period reflect Lalique's experience as a *joaillier* and others can be considered *objets vertu* in glass, designed to appeal to his established and highly discriminating patrons (Figures 29 and 30). All of the designs, however, display Lalique's mastery of glass art, including the techniques of casting, pressing, and blowing, and his full understanding of the important properties of the material.

Among Lalique's mentors in his glassmaking career was Jules Henrivaux, director of the St. Gobain Glassworks, who had labeled the twentieth century *l'age du verre*.[9] Henrivaux heralded the "age of glass" and defined the role the new material would help to play when he wrote, in 1911:

> The era of monumental art and sumptuous decor is over; it is in domestic life, in *le hôme*, that we must introduce art today, art in every form from the most modest utensil in the simplest setting to the most elaborate and luxurious of interior designs.[10]

In accordance with Henrivaux's philosophy, Lalique designed glass for *le hôme*, expanding his range to include simple, inexpensive objects which would appeal to the mass market beyond the fashionable districts of Paris and other European capitals. Among the new "Laliques" were drinking vessels and a variety of *garnitures de toilette* (Figures 31 and 33), including hand mirrors, some of which were backed with silver or bronze for stability (Figure 32). Articles for writing desk use included inkwells, blotter handles, paperweights, and seals (Figures 34 and 35).

In December 1912, three years after the opening of

*Figure 31. Box and four decorative perfume bottles in colored glass, circa 1912–1921, average height 3 in. (7.5 cm.).*

*Garnitures de toilette* in clear and colored glass were among the most attractive and popular of Lalique's products, and many designs were manufactured over a long period of years. The turquoise-colored box "4 Scarabées" (*extreme left*) was introduced in 1912 and was still available in the 1930s. *Crystal Galleries*

24 the Combs-la-Ville Glassworks, René Lalique presented his first exhibition of glass at the Place Vendôme. Promotional invitations for the event were in the form of pressed-glass medallions, molded with lettering on one side and a design of mistletoe on the verso (Figures 36 and 37). Lalique had traditionally fashioned exhibition invitations from his favorite materials (see Figure 15), and the glass medallion announced his establishment as a *maître verrier* as well as his first exhibition.

Gustave Kahn[11] described and illustrated a selection of Lalique's products, which included a variety of carafes and decanters, the majority of which were in clear glass with tall necks. Lauvrik[12] mentions "long-necked bottles" having "waterlike transparency . . . and minimal ornamentation" (Figure 38). Lalique was also making decanters in the more familiar

*Figure 32. "Narcisse Couché" hand mirror in clear and frosted glass, circa 1911–1912, engraved R. Lalique, length 11½ in. (29.5 cm.). Phillips, New York*

*Figure 33. "Papillons" (Butterflies) perfume burner in opalescent glass, circa 1912–1914, molded R. LALIQUE, height 7½ in. (19.2 cm.).*

Perfume burners are decadent boudoir accessories which were fashionable during the first quarter of this century. The object was filled with alcohol-based perfume which burned through a wick and stone, revealed when the cover was removed, filling the room with fragrance.

frosted glass by 1912, including the design known as "Masques," which is described by Lauvrik, and the "Sirènes" design (Figure 39), but he appears to have shown a preference for transparent table glass. The pear-shaped vase illustrated in Figure 40 has several features in common with this family of decanters and carafes and may date from the 1910–1914 period, although the form and signature type suggest an origin

Figure 34. "Souris" (Mice) glass seal, circa 1913, height 4¼ in. (11 cm.).

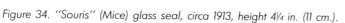

Lalique's treatment of the mice in this model is clearly inspired by the Japanese art of netsuke carving, including the characteristic method of highlighting the relief by *patine* in the recesses, which Lalique may have derived from the Oriental manner of ivory staining and his own experience of working in ivory. *Phillips, New York*

Figure 35. "Aigle" (Eagle) glass seal, circa 1913, height 3½ in. (9 cm.).

Glass seals were among the earliest of Lalique's commercially made objects. The signature on this example suggests a date of manufacture before 1914, though the model was available after World War I, when it was offered set into a rectangular standish. *Phillips, New York*

Figure 36. Invitation medallion in pea-green glass, 1912, diameter 3 in. (7.5 cm.).

This glass medallion announced René Lalique's career as a *maître verrier* as well as his first important exhibition of glass. *Crystal Galleries*

Figure 37. The opposite face of the medallion in Figure 36 is patterned with overlapping mistletoe.

*Figure 38. "Plate 2 Danseuses" carafe in clear glass, circa 1913, height 13½ in. (34 cm.).*

Lalique designed several tall-necked carafes and decanters before 1915, many of which were simple, undecorated forms with applied "handles." Glass of this type was described by Nilsen Lauvrik in 1912 as having "waterlike transparency."

*Figure 39. "Sirènes" carafe in clear glass with gray patine, circa 1911, wheel-cut R. LALIQUE, height 15¼ in. (38.7 cm.).*

This is one of René Lalique's most strikingly symbolistic designs, in which the sirens and frogs, their mouths issuing water, symbolize liquid. The form and heavy use of *patine* suggest an early date of origin, which is confirmed by the placement of the signature on the outer wall near the foot rim.

in the early 1920s.[13] The subtle, fern-leaf design is hand-engraved on the ear handles, which are free-formed and applied, as is the solid foot. A most unusual feature of the vessel is that it is free-blown, giving it all the ingredients of "studio art glass," and

suggesting it may have been made and designed by an individual craftsman.

It is somewhat ironic that René Lalique is best known today for his vases, for he did not design one for commercial production until he was over fifty, and

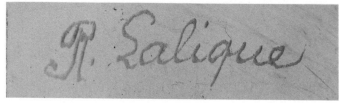

Figure 41. Detail of engraved script signature on Figure 40. This signature type was used before 1914 but is most common on glass made in the immediate postwar years.

Figure 42. "Coq" powder box and cover in black glass, circa 1910, diameter 4 in. (10.5 cm.).

In 1912, Nilsen Lauvrik described this box among Lalique glass exhibited at the Pavilion de Marsan; he admired "the incisive manner in which a cock has been cut into the cover of a pommade box . . . it has all the boldness of a vigorously executed Japanese woodcut." This example is contained in its original faux shagreen box from the Place Vendôme showroom. *Crystal Galleries*

Figure 40. Vase in free-blown glass with applied, engraved handles and foot, circa 1920–1922, engraved R. Lalique, height 9 in. (22.6 cm.).

Vases of this type are normally considered to have been made between 1912 and 1914, because of their resemblance to carafes of the period. The signature and form of this vessel, however, suggest a date of origin in the early 1920s, when similar vases were exhibited by Lalique.

the majority of them were made when he was in his sixties and seventies. Among the earliest recorded examples of mold-blown vases are two designs described by Lauvrik in 1912,[14] illustrated in Figures 44

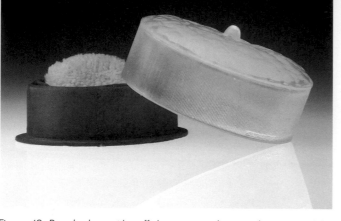

*Figure 43. Powder box with puff design in opalescent glass, circa 1912–1920, length 3½ in. (9 cm.).*

The bases of powder boxes were made in a variety of materials, including glass, metal and, as in this example, cardboard. Lauvrik wrote in 1912: "These little powder boxes may be said to epitomize the whole art of Lalique." *Crystal Galleries*

and 45. Each displays a combination of mechanical processes and handcraftsmanship in execution, characteristic of the more elaborate designs of this period, which can be considered transitional. The body of each vessel is mold-blown, probably with aid of a bellows using the *pressé soufflé* method described on page 16, and each has hand-applied decoration. The frogs and inset floral plaques recall the technique used in the *cire perdue* vessel in Figure 26 but, unlike the *cire perdue* work made contemporaneously, these vases were made in sectional molds and could be duplicated. The "frog" vase is probably unique, but Lauvrik refers to a number of blue vases of the type illustrated in Figure 44 (which is one of two examples known to the author).[15] It is likely that the vases were made in a limited series, each differing slightly from another in color or hand-applied work.

The manufacture of mold-blown vases of this proportion on a large scale required considerable technical skill and investment, largely due to the high cost of casting and installing metal molds, and only a few, smaller vases of simpler design were in mass production before 1914; the large vessels of the type in Figures 44 and 45 were made in ceramic molds.

The vase "4 Masques"[16] was among the first production vases, probably introduced late in 1912.[17] Although "4 Masques" is found only in frosted glass, a small group of vases was put into production between 1912 and 1914 in a spectrum of colors, some of which were rarely reproduced after World War I. These early models, which can be identified by an "extended L" signature (Figure 19), impressed in the center of the base, include the vase "Courges" (Figure 47), which

*Figure 44. Vase in blue glass with inlaid floral panels, circa 1912, wheel-cut R. LALIQUE, height 11½ in. (30 cm.).*

The swelling form and narrow neck of this vessel are characteristic of the prewar period. Lauvrik described vessels of this type exhibited at the Pavilion de Marsan in 1912: ". . . the large blue globular vases with their floral medallions inlaid in such a manner that they have a soft translucent light quality altogether different from the surrounding surface of the vase itself."

has the familiar bulbous form of the period and is recorded in numerous colors, including plum, turquoise, deep red, forest green, yellow, and blue. The vase illustrated in Figure 46 is also recorded with the "extended L" signature and examples exist in the rare plum color. The *monnaie du pape* leaf which decorates the vessel was a favorite of Lalique's from the 1890s and was used extensively in the interior of 40 Cours la Reine. The vase "Gui" (Figure 49) is patterned with the mistletoe favored by Lalique in his early career, and may also date from the prewar period, although no examples are known with an "elongated L" signature. A crimson red glass was used before 1914 (Figure 50), and examples of the vase "Rouces" (Fig-

Figure 45. Vase in clear glass, molded with lily pads in low relief and applied with green glass "frogs" at the shoulder, circa 1912, wheelcut R. LALIQUE, height 8¼ in. (21 cm.).

Lauvrik also mentions "a vase modeled in bold relief with frogs, frankly set on the surface." Note the swelling form, similar to that of the *cire perdue* vessel in Figure 26, and signature near the base of the vase. *Phillips, New York*

*Figure 46. "Monnaie du Pape" (Honesty Leaves) vase in opalescent glass, circa 1913–1920, molded R. LALIQUE, height 9¼ in (23 cm.).*

The heavy *patine*, characteristic of the early period of manufacture, was achieved by covering the vessel with an enamel solution which was wiped away from the relief surfaces when it began to dry and fixed with a low-temperature muffle firing. *Phillips, New York*

ure 48) are recorded in this color. The form and decoration of the "Rouces" model also suggest that it belongs to the prewar family of vases.

René Lalique used colored glass in his smaller glass objects and *garnitures de toilette* as well as in vase designs (Figure 51). Black glass was preferred for seals, inkwells, boxes, and more expensive perfume bottles, and a turquoise color was occasionally employed, mostly for boxes. The frosted glass that became Lalique's trademark was most common, often used in combination with clear, polished areas.

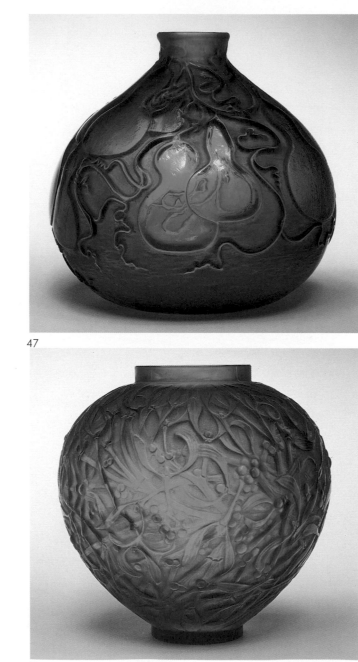

47

48

49

*Figure 47. "Courges" (Gourds) vase in blue glass, circa 1913, molded R. LALIQUE, with "extended L," height 6½ in. (16.6 cm.).*

The organic form and decoration of this vessel are evidence of its early origin. "Courges" may have been the first of Lalique's production vases made in colored glass. *Collection of Mr. and Mrs. V. James Cole*

*Figure 48. "Rouces" (Briars) vase in green glass, circa 1913–1920, molded R. LALIQUE, height 9 in. (23 cm.).*

The entwined-briar motif appears on several of Lalique's early glass designs and was first used on the stoppers of perfume bottles designed for François Coty (Figure 18). *Collection of Mr. and Mrs. V. James Cole*

*Figure 49. "Gui" (Mistletoe) vase in blue glass, circa 1913–1920, molded R. LALIQUE, height 6½ in. (17 cm.).*

The mistletoe that patterns "Gui" was first used on glass by Lalique in 1912 (Figure 37). *Collection of Mr. and Mrs. V. James Cole*

At Clairfontaine, Lalique continued to cast decorative glass panels for use in architecture, all of which were made in frosted glass. Among the commissions he undertook in the immediate prewar years was the manufacture of floral windows for the New York premises of his friend and collaborator, François Coty, located at 714 Fifth Avenue. The panels, which were made in 1912 under the auspices of the Union Centrale des Arts Décoratifs, were probably installed before the opening of the Coty showroom in 1913, and can still be admired at the time of writing. In the same year, Lalique cast decorative glass panels with figural design which were incorporated into a pair of wrought-iron gates designed by Bellery Desfontaines,[18] and one surviving panel is recorded.[19] The gate panels, molded with allegorical figures of the Seasons, are typical of Lalique's architectural work cast at Clairfontaine, most of which is in the form of classical friezes or bas-reliefs.

*Figure 50. "Hirondelles" (Swallows) vase in crimson-colored glass, circa 1913, impressed Lalique with "extended L," height 9¼ in. (23.5 cm.).*

*Red glass was used by Lalique before World War I and this example probably dates from that period, although the design, which is also known in gray and clear glass, was manufactured into the 1920s. Phillips, New York*

# 3. THE IRREPRESSIBLE CREATOR (1915–1930)

World War I forced Lalique to cease glass production at Combs-la-Ville in 1915. When the factory reopened in 1919 the rapid growth which had characterized Lalique's glass empire before the war also resumed. The immediate postwar years witnessed a new liberalism in art and culture, evidenced by the exaggerated importance of elegance and "chic," and encouraged by an affluent society and a new leisure class in Europe and the Americas. With competition from German glassmakers temporarily removed, Lalique strategically fed his designs to an international public hungry for French decorative art, interior design, tableware, and toiletries.

In 1919 Lalique exhibited extensively at galleries and museums in several countries, including a large display at the Museum of Industrial Arts in Copenhagen, and in June of that year he mounted two debut exhibitions in New York, held simultaneously at Knoedler Galleries and the Brooklyn Museum. The latter exhibition included twenty-eight production designs: necklaces, *bonbonnières*, paperweights, powder boxes, seals, and statuettes,[1] most of which were probably designed before 1914. In addition, a number of *cire perdue* vases were shown.

The making of *cire perdue* glass increased in scale and importance after 1919, and postwar examples are normally marked and thus easily identifiable. The mark consists of a control number of simple consecutive progression followed by a slash and the last two digits of the year of manufacture. Thus, the majority of *cire perdue* ware made after 1919 can be dated to the year of manufacture and, by recording the marks on numerous examples of *cire perdue*, the number of pieces made in any given year can be calculated with a reasonable degree of accuracy. The earliest postwar model known to the author is the figure of a crouching cougar illustrated in Figure 53, which is inscribed with the numbers 25–19. Assuming the system began with number 1, the numbers on recorded examples of *cire perdue*, including several illustrated in *Lalique Glass*, indicate that production continued until about 1929[2] and was at a rate of approximately seventy new designs per annum.

Given this level of output, it is unlikely that many of the wax *maquettes* for the dated *cire perdue* ware were modeled by René Lalique. The numerals were incised into the *maquette*, unlike the signature, which was added to the finished product at a final quality control stage, usually by a wheel-cutting technique. There are exceptions to the numbering system, including unsigned examples and other anomalies, but the majority of numbered examples conform, most of them dating between 1919 and 1926.[3] Five examples of dated *cire perdue* ware are illustrated (Figures 53, 60, 62, 189, and 198).

Throughout the first half of the 1920s Lalique's *cire*

32

Figure 51. "2 Sirènes" box in orange glass, circa 1920, molded R. LALIQUE, diameter 10¼ in. (26.3 cm.).

*Bonbonnières* were among Lalique's most popular products in the early 1920s and 1930s and examples were first exhibited in America at the Brooklyn Museum in 1919. *Crystal Galleries*

led to a new era of expansion for the Lalique Company and the French decorative glass industry in general. A new glassworks was planned and work began in 1919 at a site in the Alsace region of France, a former German province to which industry was attracted by government incentives offered after the war. Lalique's factory, completed in 1921, was located in the small town of Wingen-sur-Moder, and has continued to provide the main source of employment for the inhabitants of Wingen to the present day.

The expansion of production facilities coincided with a growth in Lalique's network of retail outlets, which had been limited to the Place Vendôme showroom and a few exclusive jewelry stores in European capitals before the war. In the early 1920s Lalique es-

Figure 52. "Lézards" paperweight in clear glass, circa 1914.

The signature on this example was in use before World War I but most commonly used on glass made in the immediate postwar years.

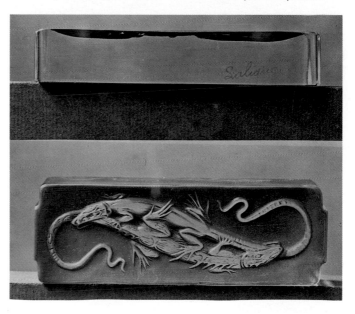

*perdue* glass was prominently displayed at exhibitions which, as Henrivaux observed, "exerted a considerable influence on public taste and provided creative inspiration for the exhibitors."[4] Some vases were exhibited over a number of years and ultimately acquired by Lalique's wealthier and more discriminating private patrons or by museums[5] (Figure 61).

The Combs-la-Ville Glassworks was adequately equipped to produce the *cire perdue* work: perfume bottles, desk and dressing table items, table glass, and the few vase designs which constituted Lalique's range of output in 1919. The growing international market, coupled with what William Morris called "the irrepressible longing for creation" of René Lalique,

34

*Figure 53. Figure of a crouching cougar in cire perdue glass, 1919, wheel-cut R. LALIQUE and incised 25–19, height 6 in. (15 cm.).*

The yellow ocher staining is highly effective on this model. Note the characteristic rough, matte, pitted surface and the numerous fingerprint impressions. *Phillips, New York*

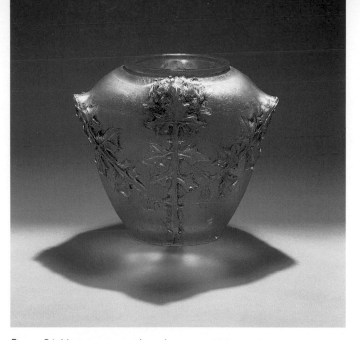

*Figure 54. Vase in* cire perdue *glass, circa 1913–1920, inscribed Lalique, height 10 in. (25.5 cm.).*

Vases of this type, exhibited at the Brooklyn Museum, were described in *The International Studio* in June 1919: "[The vases'] beauty depends upon form and design more than upon color, which is frequently that of clear glass, but occasionally of a light copper-colored stain said to be a form of enamel." *Robert Gingold Collection. Photo: William Doyle Galleries*

tablished agents and suitable outlets throughout France and in several foreign countries, including England, Argentina, and the United States. The American department stores proved particularly suitable for Lalique as they were well equipped to import large quantities of glass, were established in regional networks, and enjoyed a high level of prestige. Ovington's, the East Coast chain, began offering Lalique glass in their New York headquarters in 1924, and by the end of the decade Lalique was available in most regions of the United States through a network of stores from Wanamaker's in Philadelphia to Alexander and Oviatt's in Los Angeles.

At Wingen Lalique entered a new era of modernism in decorative glass manufacture. The facility allowed him to fulfill his ideal of producing high-quality designs at modest prices for use in *le hôme*, a goal that provided much of the impetus in his career. Maximilian Gauthier recorded Lalique's objectives at Wingen during an interview with him in 1925:

> [Lalique's goals were] to reduce the price of his glass while multiplying and diversifying designs, and to introduce his art into every household by making it available to everyone.[6]

*Figure 55. Vase in* cire perdue *glass, circa 1919, wheel-cut R. LALIQUE, height 12½ in. (32 cm.).*

This model is not marked with incised numerals, is of unusually large size, and of a design that could be duplicated by a conventional sectional mold—all indications that it may have been a prototype or suggestion for a production vessel. (Compare with Figures 65, 80, and 99.)

36 *Figure 56. Vase in cire perdue glass, circa 1921, height 7½ in. (19 cm.).*

The first evidence of symmetry in Lalique's designs appears in his *cire perdue* work of the early 1920s. This design may have inspired the popular production vase "Ceylan" (Figure 59). *Calouste Gulbenkian Museum, Lisbon*

*Figure 57. Vase in cire perdue glass circa 1913, height 4½ in. (11.5 cm.).*

Lalique designed a variety of small *cire perdue* vessels applied with bats, moths, and other winged insects in high relief; the results inspired a number of production designs, including the inkwell in Figure 58. *Calouste Gulbenkian Museum, Lisbon*

*Figure 58. "3 Papillons" (Butterflies) inkwell in clear and frosted glass, circa 1914–1920, height 3 in. (7.5 cm.).*

The design of this model is clearly inspired by Lalique's *cire perdue* work. This example is a modified version of the design dating from the early 1930s; the earlier version is more fluently modeled and fitted with a flat cover. *Phillips, New York*

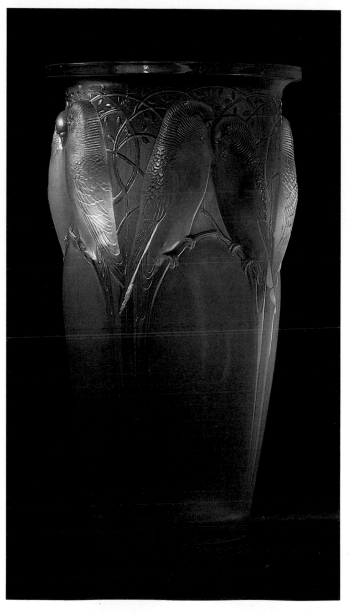

Figure 59. "Ceylan" vase in opalescent glass, circa 1922, wheel-cut R. LALIQUE FRANCE, height 10 in. (25.5 cm.).

Figure 60. Ashtray in cire perdue glass, 1920, engraved Lalique and incised 191–20, diameter 6½ in. (16.8 cm.).

The majority of Lalique's postwar *cire perdue* work consists of vase designs, though a few ashtrays are recorded, mostly incorporating charming animal figurines. *Phillips, New York*

Between 1920 and 1930 Lalique tripled his work force and increased glass production tenfold. Working alone from his Paris atelier he designed an astonishing number and variety of articles for an insatiable public and an increasing number of commercial patrons. His products were as diverse as the ideas that inspired them. In the rest of this chapter, each category of ware will be discused under subheadings, beginning with Lalique's most successful and best-known product—the decorative vase.

## Vases

Among the earliest products of the new factory were a number of large, mold-blown vases of bulbous or Japanese form. The vases were manufactured in clear, opalescent, or colored glass, sometimes decorated with *patine* of one or more colors (Figure 73). The earliest examples, dating from 1920 and 1921, are decorated with random, organic, or naturalistic patterns evocative of Lalique's earlier work (Figure 67) and are

*Figure 61. Vase in* cire perdue *glass, circa 1921, height 10 in. (25.5 cm.).*

Lalique's *cire perdue* work played an important role at exhibitions throughout the first half of the 1920s. This example was exhibited at the Pavilion de Marsan in 1922 and again at the Paris Exposition of 1925. A very similar model, decorated with four pairs of birds, was displayed at the Brooklyn Museum in 1919 and illustrated in the *American Magazine of Art*, June 1919, p. 301. *Calouste Gulbenkian Museum, Lisbon*

sometimes marked with the engraved script signature found on a variety of Lalique glass objects made in the immediate postwar years (Figure 66). The vase "Sauterelles" (Figures 63 and 64), described by Miguel Zamacoïs as "a vase whereupon huge grasshoppers perch on sinuous reeds," [7] was one of the first large vases made at Wingen. The design remained in production until about 1930 and was made in a spectrum of colors in the late 1920s.

*Figure 62. Vase in* cire perdue *glass, 1923, wheel-cut R. LALIQUE and incised 437–23, height 7½ in. (19.5 cm.).*

The grotesque, bullheaded fish which decorate this vessel are distinctively Lalique, strangely modeled overlapping and vertical, the lips meeting at the base, the protruding eyes forming feet.

*Figure 63. "Sauterelles" vase in green glass, engraved R. Lalique France No. 888, height 10 in. (25.5 cm.).*

The popular "Grasshoppers" model was made in a spectrum of colors during the late 1920s. The signature type on this example suggests a date of manufacture after 1925. *Collection of Mr. and Mrs. V. James Cole*

Figure 64. "Sauterelles" (Grasshoppers) vase in clear glass with blue and green patine, circa 1922, engraved Lalique, height 10 in. (25.5 cm.).

This popular design was manufactured throughout the 1920s, but the coloration and signature type on this example suggest it is an early model (see Figure 66). *Collection of Robert and Karen Ettinger*

The impressive proportions of Lalique's vases (the largest was over 16 inches tall, Figure 65) were a response to the demands of a new generation of French interior designers, who worked under the auspices of design ateliers such as Primavera or leading Parisian department stores. Among the foremost *maîtres de l'oeuvre* in the early 1920s were Maurice Dufrène, Paul Follot, and Emile-Jacques Ruhlmann, all of whom combined their own talents with those of young and

Figure 66. *Engraved signature in script which appears on a variety of Lalique glass products of the immediate postwar years. An initial "R" is sometimes present. Crystal Galleries*

Figure 65. *"Palestre" vase in frosted glass, circa 1922, wheel-cut R. LALIQUE, height 16½ in. (42 cm.).*

This monumental vessel was the largest of Lalique's production designs. *Bonhams, London*

Figure 67. *"Grande Boule Lierre" (Ivy) vase, circa 1921, wheel-cut R. LALIQUE FRANCE, height 13½ in. (35 cm.). Phillips, New York*

aspiring *artistes décorateurs*, creating decor to suit the rhythm of modern life while retaining the standards, taste, and richness of an elegant past. Lalique's larger vases, as well as his *surtouts* of the late 1920s, complemented these interiors and found widespread popu-

larity (Figures 68, 69, 70, and 75). The majority of larger vases are simply decorated forms of molded pattern with little or no surface treatment. During the early years at Wingen, however, Lalique experimented with a variety of techniques for decorating mold-blown vessels. The vases illustrated in Figure 76 have identical bodies, blown in the same mold, and applied handles. The use of standard "blank" bodies reduced the unit cost of each vessel, which was largely

*Figure 68. "Lézards et Bleuets" (Lizards and Cornflowers) vase in black glass, molded R. LALIQUE, height 13¼ in. (34 cm.).*

Many of Lalique's larger vases were designed to complement contemporary interior design. This model is one of the few production vases made in black glass and was also made in clear (white) glass (Figure 69). Collection of Robert and Karen Ettinger

*Figure 69. "Lézards et Bleuets" vase in clear and frosted glass, circa 1922. Collection of Robert and Karen Ettinger*

*Figure 70. "Languedoc" vase in green glass, circa 1925, engraved R. Lalique France, height 9 in. (22.5 cm.).*

Heavily walled vessels such as this one were made possible by the automated blowing processes used at the Wingen Glassworks. *Gallerie Moderne*

Figure 71. "Sophora" vase in pale gray glass with gray patination, circa 1925, engraved R. Lalique France No. 997, height 10¼ in. (26 cm.).

A prototype of this design was made in black glass in 1925 with acid-etched decoration. The technique of polishing raised areas of a pattern and "reserving" against a frosted or patinated ground was a favorite of René Lulique's. *Collection of A. J. Tobias*

*Figure 72. "Senlis" vase in deep violet glass with bronze handles, circa 1926, height 10¼ in. (26 cm.).*

The blank body that inspired "Sophora" (Figure 71) was used in this model and another massive vessel with bronze mounts titled "Cluny" (Design No. 961). *Weinstein Collection*

*Figure 73. "Sauge" (Sage) vase in pale amber glass, circa 1920, molded R. LALIQUE, height 10 in. (25.5 cm.).*

Lalique was fascinated with patterns of overlapping leafage, depicted naturalistically on this early vase design. The heavy use of *patine* gives this example an autumnal appeal. *Collection of A. J. Tobias*

*Figure 75. "Alicante" vase in blue glass, circa 1924, engraved R. Lalique France No. 998, height 10 in. (25.5 cm.).*

This design, with its striking pattern of tropical birds, is typical of the decorated Japanese forms Lalique produced in a spectrum of colors throughout the 1920s and early 1930s. *Collection of A. J. Tobias*

*Figure 74. "Gros Scarabées" vase in deep amber glass, circa 1926, molded R. LALIQUE, height 11½ in. (29 cm.). Collection of Dr. Donald Gutfriend*

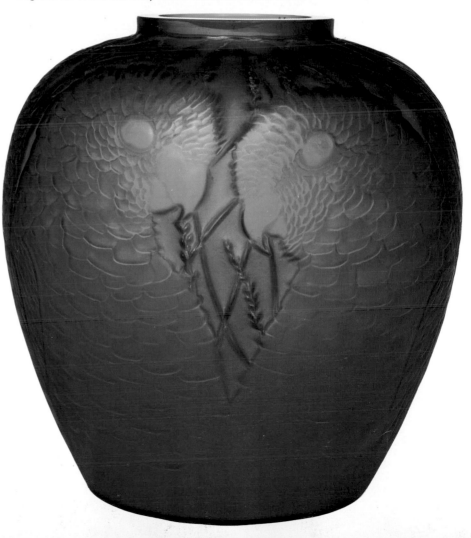

*Figure 76. "2 Oiseaux" (Birds) and "Grenouilles" (Frogs) vases in clear and frosted glass, circa 1922, height 10¼ in. (26 cm.).*

A few vase designs with applied decoration on "blank" bodies were introduced in the early 1920s but met with limited commercial success.

The vases were in black glass, decorated with geometrically stylized foliate patterns of vertical emphasis in shallow, acid-etched relief.[3] No surviving examples of these vases are known and they may have been made as prototypes, which would explain why each model was allocated the same design number and distinguished by a supplementary letter. The production vase "Sophora" (Figure 71) is of identical form and design to one of the acid-etched series, and may have been put into production as the most popular model. The blank body was used for two extraordinary vases mounted with bronze handles, which are among Lalique's most powerful vase designs (Figure 72).

A few other rare examples of acid-etched designs from the 1920s are recorded, including an amphora-form vessel titled "Radio" (design number 1009), with

absorbed in the expensive steel molds, while allowing for diversity in design by "grafting on" inexpensively cast work. Despite these advantages, production of vases of this type was on a small scale and discontinued by the mid-1920s, largely because each model required more production stages and hand finishing than the simple, mold-blown designs. Throughout his career Lalique avoided designs that required numerous stages in manufacture; production vessels with this characteristic are uncommon.

Another technique that Lalique experimented with was the use of etching with hydrofluoric acid, which was popularized in the 1920s by the Daum brothers' glassworks. In 1925 a series of six vases was introduced as design numbers 885B through 885G, molded as blanks of bulbous form with widely everted rims.

*Figure 77. "Téhéran" vase in clear glass, circa 1924, molded R. LALIQUE, engraved France.*

The Persian-style "Téhéran" is the only Lalique production vase of the 1920s with acid-etched decoration. In contrast to the monolithic vases made contemporaneously, this tiny vessel is only 3½ in. (8 cm.) in height.

a pattern of zigzag flashes, which was introduced in 1925.[9] The technique was successfully used on only one production vessel in the 1920s; the tiny vase "Téhéran" (Figure 77), which was probably designed in 1924. During the 1930s a number of vases were introduced with this form of decoration.

The cost of casting the steel molds required for Lalique's large vase designs was extremely high in the 1920s,[10] and their installation and successful application required considerable skill and innovative technology. Much of the success in production levels and quality control at the Wingen factory was due to the efforts of René Lalique's son, Marc Lalique (1900–1977), who was given the responsibility of managing the plant when he joined the company in 1922.

In contrast to his father, Marc Lalique developed the skills of engineering and applied technology, introducing a series of improvements in glassmaking machinery throughout the 1920s, many of which were subsequently patented. The manufacture of Lalique's designs presented a variety of problems, most of them at the critical annealing, or cooling, stage of the process. Large, heavy vessels were inclined to sag and become misshapen under their own weight if released too rapidly from the protection of a mold, while designs with variable thicknesses of glass were liable to crack or even explode if annealed too quickly. The observance of critical temperatures and annealing times was imperative, and much of Marc Lalique's work was concentrated in these areas. His innovations included the use of hot air in automatic blowing, revolving molds, which reduced the incidence of malformation, and the controlled heating of metal molds to prevent adherence to the glass and aid in the annealing process.

Many of the smaller vases were mouth-blown, at both Combs-la-Ville and Wingen, where all the large designs were made in semiautomated molds. The new processes permitted the blowing of heavily walled vessels which could not have been made by traditional mouth-blowing. Lalique exploited this advantage by designing bold, heavy vessels and introducing "casing," or layering, to effect opacity or enhance the translucent properties of colored glass. Casing was achieved by applying two, or sometimes three, separate gathers of molten glass, one over the

*Figure 78. "Acacia" vase in charcoal-gray glass, circa 1923, molded R. LALIQUE, height 8 in. (20 cm.).*

Many of Lalique's smaller vases were blown by mouth into molds. *Souffleurs* worked at both of the Lalique glassworks during the interwar period and are still employed at Wingen to blow glass in the traditional manner.

46

*Figure 79. "Alicante" vase in double-cased jade-green glass, circa 1925, engraved R. Lalique France, height 10¼ in. (26 cm.).*

"Casing" is the name given to the technique of blowing one or more "gathers" of glass into a mold simultaneously, one on top of the other, which Lalique used to effect semiopacity or opalescence in colored glass. Three layers of glass have been used in this "double-cased" example, two of jade-green color and an opalescent layer sandwiched between them, clearly visible on the sheared neck of the vessel.

*Figure 80. "Archers" vase in blue glass, circa 1923, molded R. LALIQUE, height 10¼ in. (26 cm.).*

This bright "electric" blue was one of the most successful of Lalique's range of colors in the 1920s. *Weinstein Collection*

*Figure 81. "Tourbillons" (Whirlwinds) vase in amber glass, circa 1925, stenciled R. LALIQUE FRANCE, height 8 in. (20 cm.).*

*Figure 82. "Tourbillons" vase in turquoise-blue glass, wheel-cut R. LALIQUE FRANCE. Weinstein Collection*

other, onto the pontil rod, or blowing tube, and introducing the combined gather into the mold, rather like blowing up two different-colored balloons at once, one inside the other (Figure 79).

The most important technical development at the Wingen Glassworks was the introduction of the press-molding method of manufacture, which was first used in 1921. The process, used only at Wingen, allowed the manufacture of hollowware without blowing glass, which was forced into the mold by a vertical plunger. The presses, some of which are still in use, resemble old-fashioned printing presses, operated by a simple lever system. Shortly after its introduction the press-molding system was described in the magazine *Mobilier et Décoration*:

> Lalique makes use of the glass-pressing process for production designs. The molten glass is poured directly into a steel mold from the crucible, wherein it is forcibly compounded by means of a press. On contact with the wall of the mold, the glass cools and retracts slightly; at this point the mold is quickly opened to avoid the danger of cracking; not too quickly, however, as the still semimolten glass is at risk of becoming malformed. The operation, as we have observed it, requires a skillful "turn of hand."[11]

The skillful turn of hand was provided by one or two men, depending on the weight of glass required in the vessel design.

A characteristic feature of vases made on a press is that the mouth of the vessel is the widest part of the body, thus allowing for the entry and retraction of the plunger. All pressed designs, therefore, taper downward to some degree and are distinct from mold-blown vessels, which are typically bulbous and narrow-necked (Figure 85). Another distinguishing feature of pressed vases is an even inner surface, un-

*Figure 83. "Moissac" vase in blue glass, circa 1925, wheel-cut R. LALIQUE FRANCE, height 5¼ in. (13.3 cm.).*

All vessels made by the press technique taper downward to some degree in order to allow the entry and retraction of the plunger which forced the molten glass into the mold. Lalique designed a variety of vases of simple but effective conical form which could be manufactured cheaply and easily by this method. *Collection of A. J. Tobias*

*Figure 84. "Pierrefonds" vase in amber glass, circa 1926, stenciled R. LALIQUE FRANCE, length across handles 13½ in. (34 cm.).*

Some of Lalique's boldest designs date from the first five years of operation of the Wingen factory, when the press-molding technique was developed. The extreme pressure under which the molten glass was forced into the mold allowed for sharply defined, solid areas of glass and a variation in relief which could not be achieved by conventional or semiautomated methods of blowing. *Collection of A. J. Tobias*

Figure 85. "Eucalyptus" vase in purplish glass, circa 1922, molded R. LALIQUE, height 6½ in. (16.5 cm.).

This model is one of Lalique's earliest designs for press manufacture and is rarely found in colored glass. *Collection of Mr. and Mrs. V. James Cole*

production at Wingen. Many of the designs remained in production for extended periods of time, a reflection of their popularity and a trend encouraged by the high cost of metal molds. Lalique continued to introduce new models and, after about 1926, most of them were designed for press manufacture, which was less expensive and less complicated than mold-blowing and resulted in a lower percentage of "wasters."

Despite the large numbers of imitators and competitors, Lalique's vases are the finest of the genre, especially those produced in colored glass. Their design, execution, and overall quality were unmatched in the 1920s and have not been equaled since.

## Statuary, Cast Glass, and the 1925 Exposition

Lalique's processes for casting glass for use in solid, sculptural, and architectural work were also greatly improved at Wingen. Prior to the opening of the new works, sculptural work had been mostly in miniature, limited to figural seals, stoppers, etc., and some *cire perdue* work. Within a year of operations, however, Lalique was sculpting glass on a larger scale, creating

like blown ware in which the inner surface often follows the contours of exterior relief decoration.

Some of René Lalique's finest designs resulted from the use of the press in the early and mid-1920s, despite the stylistic limitations presented by the technique (Figures 81, 82, and 84).

Lalique designed more than two hundred vases between 1920 and 1930, most of which were put into

Figure 86. Wheel-cut signature of the type used on vases made on the press and a few large mold-blown vases in the 1920s. The signature is sometimes accompanied by the word FRANCE and an engraved design number.

three-dimensional forms of favorite images he had previously depicted only in shallow relief.

Among the earliest and most successful results of this new genre was the celebrated statuette "Suzanne" (Figure 100), the first examples of which were made in 1922.[12] The majority of "Suzanne" models were in frosted or opalescent glass (which was used in over 90 percent of Lalique's production ware of the 1920s and 1930s), though examples are sometimes found in an amber color. "Suzanne" and the companion figure "Thaïs" (Figure 102) were manufactured until the mid-1930s.

Lalique's translucent glass statuary was ideally displayed under illumination, from either behind or underneath, and several statuettes were available with decorative bronze illuminating stands (Figure 101) to facilitate illumination and create the spectacular results which were described by Miguel Zamacoïs as "*divinement lumineux.*"[13]

Lalique's cast work became increasingly ambitious during the 1920s. In 1922 he designed a model of a gigantic deep-sea fish, to be cast in solid glass. Entitled "Gros Poisson," the figure was made in opalescent and clear glass.[14] The following year a new version of the model was introduced entitled "Gros Poisson Vagues" (Figure 105), which was probably the result of modifying the earlier mold, and the first version was discontinued. The huge fish, made only in clear glass, was mounted for effective display on a

*Figure 87. Full signature in engraved script of the type added to much of Lalique's blown-glass products from about 1924 to the mid-1930s.*

*Figure 88. "Tortues" (Tortoises) vase in clear and frosted glass, circa 1924, height 10½ in. (26.5 cm.).*

Miguel Zamacoïs admired this model at the Place Vendôme showroom in 1928: "What strength and audacity in the superb vase, composed entirely of tortoises arranged one over the other, their shells forming a regular pattern." From *Chez René Lalique,* by Miguel Zamacoïs (Paris, 1928).

Figure 89. "Rampillons" vase in purple glass, circa 1926, wheel-cut R. LALIQUE FRANCE, height 5 in. (12.8 cm.).

The use of purple glass is extremely rare, especially in small production vases. *Weinstein Collection*

Figure 90. "Pétrarque" vase in purplish glass, circa 1927, wheel-cut R. LALIQUE, height 8½ in. (22 cm.).

The press-molding technique allowed Lalique to manufacture massive vases of bold design. The walls of this example are almost one inch in thickness. *Weinstein Collection*

Figure 91. "Malesherbes" vase in mint-green glass, circa 1926, engraved R. Lalique France No. 7074, height 9 in. (23 cm.).

The decoration on "Malesherbes" is typical of Lalique's transitional stage between naturalistic and fully stylized treatment of foliage. *Collection of Mr. and Mrs. V. James Cole*

Figure 92. "Borromée" vase in violet glass, circa 1927, stenciled R. LALIQUE FRANCE, height 9 in. (23 cm.).

The design, execution, and overall quality of Lalique's vases were unparalleled and without precedent in the 1920s and have not been equaled since. *Collection of Lee and Jane Kolczun*

Figure 93. ''Ferrières'' vase in green glass, circa 1926, engraved R. Lalique France No. 1019, height 6½ in. (17 cm.).

Figure 94. ''Albert'' vase in blue glass, circa 1927, stenciled R. LALIQUE FRANCE, height 6½ in. (17 cm.).

The majority of Lalique's vases designed after 1925 were for press manufacture. Collection of Mr. and Mrs. V. James Cole

bronze illuminating stand of Japanese pattern. The process of casting figures of this scale was described in the magazine *Artwork* in 1927:

> Lalique's figure work is cast in great molds of steel, prepared very much as are the molds for bronzes. The ''metal'' is poured in molten and in this way pieces of far greater size and importance are produced than is possible under other methods.[15]

Figure 95. ''Escargot'' (Snail) vase in red glass, circa 1920, molded R. LALIQUE, height 8½ in. (22 cm.). Collection of Mr. and Mrs. V. James Cole

*Figure 96. "Marguerites" vase in cased white glass, circa 1924, engraved R. Lalique France No. 922, height 8¼ in. (21 cm.).*

Lalique made effective use of enameling on several designs of the mid-1920s, highlighting relief in either matte-black, blue, or brown. "Marguerites" is one of a small number of production vases made in opaque white glass.

Thus, the technique of casting glass in metal molds, which was first demonstrated by Ringel in the 1890s and which Lalique had employed since his experiments at Clairfontaine, was perfected at the Wingen Glassworks. In the early 1920s Lalique designed a number of figures of comparable scale to

"Gros Poisson Vagues," including a companion piece ("Gros Poisson Algues"), and several female nudes. Production of architectural panels, which were made in the same technique, was greatly increased, and the new facility allowed him to undertake large and ambitious architectural projects, including exterior design and the manufacture of glass furniture, which was produced in limited quantities from the mid-1920s, often to special commission. Architectural or furniture panels could be purchased individually in the Place Vendôme showroom in the mid-1920s,[16] but were normally incorporated into commissioned work (Figures 104 and 106).

Despite the staggering variety and scale of Lalique's output, his glass retained the consistency in quality and style which had been responsible for its initial success. This was achieved by Lalique's determination to continue as the company's sole designer

*Figure 97. "Poivre" (Pepper Plant) vase in clear and frosted glass, circa 1922, molded R. LALIQUE, height 9¼ in. (23.5 cm.). Phillips, New York*

Figure 98. "Camées" (Cameos) vase in clear and frosted glass, circa 1929, engraved R. Lalique France No. 891, height 10 in. (25.5 cm.). Phillips, New York

designs, a policy that did not conform to traditional methods of commercial glass production. This dilemma was recorded in *Artwork*:

> The despair of good business heads, Lalique's trouble is his own fertility of ideas. They come too quickly, they jostle one another so freely that before one has been made to yield the profit of which it is capable, the next is clamoring for attention.[17]

Lalique found an important forum for his new designs at national and international exhibitions, which revived in popularity after World War I. New creations, together with established successes and *cire perdue* work, were also widely shown at the Paris salons, including the important salon of the Société des Artistes Décorateurs, held twice annually at the Pavilion de Marsan (in the Musée des Arts Décoratifs). Many of Lalique's glassmaking contemporaries worked in "studio" conditions, creating unique works or designs made in limited series. Among the most popular and respected members of this group were Maurice Marinot, Gabriel Argy-Rousseau, and Jean Sala, who ex-

Figure 99. "Lutteurs" (Wrestlers) vase in clear and frosted glass, circa 1920, molded R. LALIQUE, height 5¼ in. (13.5 cm.). Phillips, New York

and, in contrast to many of his glassmaking contemporaries, Lalique refused the temptation to overexploit his talents by copying and reworking designs with proven commercial appeal, or to jeopardize the quality of production to reduce unit costs and increase sales.

Despite his reclusive lifestyle, René Lalique remained very much in touch with the modern world and steadily introduced new—and often daring—

hibited alongside René Lalique in the 1920s and received equal attention by contemporary critics, despite the fundamental difference in approach to design and manufacturing techniques.

The most important exhibition was the Exposition des Arts Décoratifs et Industriels, held in Paris in the summer of 1925. Twenty-one foreign countries participated in the Exposition but the event was principally a showcase of French decorative art. Lalique's glass was in evidence throughout the site: Visitors were welcomed through a magnificent *porte d'honneur* which was flanked by panels of Lalique's frosted glass (the effect of the panels was somewhat depleted at night

*Figure 101. During the mid-1920s "Suzanne" was available with a decorative bronze illuminating stand. The high cost of the stands, equal to the cost of the glass figure, made them commercially unsuccessful and accounts for their rarity today. A plain metal stand was introduced in the late 1920s.*

*Figure 100. "Suzanne" statuette in opalescent glass, circa 1922, molded R. LALIQUE, height 9 in. (23 cm.).*

The diaphanous gown and sensuous form of "Suzanne" are delightfully enhanced by the effect of light transmitted through the opalescent glass.

Figure 102. "Thaïs" statuette in opalescent glass, circa 1923, wheel-cut R. LALIQUE, height 9 in. (23 cm.).

The companion figure to "Suzanne" is equally graceful and the rarer of the two models. *Phillips, New York*

Lalique's own displays were housed in a starkly modernist pavilion, designed by him in collaboration with the architect Marc Ducluzand (Figure 108), which stood among pavilions sponsored by Parisian department stores and established companies, including Christofle, Baccarat, and Sèvres. Lalique's pavilion contained a large quantity of *cire perdue* glass, together with a number of unique exhibition pieces, including a monumental vase, over six feet high, and a single example of early jewelry.[18]

Lalique was able to reserve the pavilion as a showpiece of *cire perdue* since his production ware was dis-

Figure 103. "Figurine avec Guirlande de Fruits," in frosted glass, circa 1924, molded R. LALIQUE, height 8¼ in. (21 cm.). *Crystal Galleries*

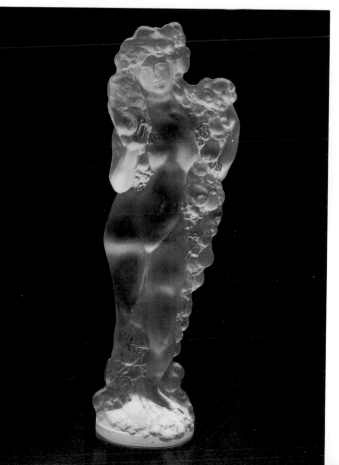

by the architect's decision not to illuminate them from behind, as was Lalique's original intention). The centerpiece was a colossal Lalique fountain, over forty feet in height, of octagonal sections, built of frosted glass panels in seventeen tiers, each of which was mounted with eight "Source de la Fontaine" statuettes (Figure 107).

*Figure 104. Decorative panel in frosted glass, circa 1925, 12½ in. × 6¼ in. (33 cm.×16 cm.).*

Panels of this type, intended for vertical display, have "V" grooved edges to facilitate slotting into a metal frame. *Collection of Glenn and Mary Lou Utt*

played throughout the exhibition and in a small showroom, one of seven built on the Pont Alexandre II, where vases, bowls, and table glass were shown.[19]

Many of Lalique's large vases and lighting fixtures were included in room settings exhibited by *ensembliers*, or in the Art et Décoration building, which featured a cross-section of contemporary French decorative arts. Lalique was commissioned to decorate a modernist dining room, housed in the Sèvres pavilion, which included an illuminated ceiling in frosted glass and was considered one of the most successful

*Figure 105. "Gros Poisson Vagues" (Large Fish, Waves) in clear glass with bronze illuminating stand, circa 1923, wheel-cut R. LALIQUE FRANCE, height 15½ in. (39.5 cm.).*

The improvements in the casting of glass in hollow molds, developed at the Wingen Glassworks, allowed Lalique to cast sculptural designs of this scale by the early 1920s. The "slippery" appearance of the fish was achieved by smoothing the surfaces of the model and polishing it to a high sheen.

*Figure 106. Breakfast table in glass and metal by Lalique and Sabino, height 55 in. (140 cm.).*

Lalique tables were often illuminated from within. This example was made for the couturier Jean Lanvin in 1937. *Christie's, New York*

and accomplished displays of the exhibition. The perfume company Roger et Gallet also employed Lalique's talents as an interior designer, and its entire stand in the *parfumerie* section was designed by him, including the vitrines, furniture, and perfume containers.

Lalique's bottles were prominently displayed in the *parfumerie* section, located on the Grand Palais, which was dominated by a magnificent "Fontaine des Parfums" (Figure 109).

René Lalique was sixty-five years old in 1925 and a veteran of decorative arts exhibitions. His contributions confirmed his position of supremacy in decorative glass design and manufacture and demon-

strated his remarkable range of talents and abilities to an optimum degree. The flood of criticism and commentary which coincided with the event contained no adverse reaction to Lalique's work. Maximilian Gauthier, who wrote in a less embellished style than most of his colleagues, noted:

> Lalique makes clean, industrially produced designs for people of modern taste and modest income. . . . He will certainly be considered, by the historians of the next century, as one of the foremost figures in the modern renaissance of French applied arts.[20]

*Figure 108. Lalique's pavilion at the 1925 Exposition, designed by René Lalique and Marc Ducluzand.*

The doors of the pavilion were composed of 2,000 pieces of glass. Inside, the display consisted mostly of *cire perdue* glass arranged in vitrines around a monumental freestanding vase, over six feet in height, constructed of frosted glass panels molded with acanthus leaves and prancing horses.

*Figure 107. "Source de la Fontaine" statuette in frosted glass, circa 1925, wheel-cut R. LALIQUE, height 21½ in. (55 cm.) total.*

Lalique's fountain at the 1925 Exposition was mounted with 136 "Source de la Fontaine" statuettes, of which thirteen versions were made in three sizes. *Bonhams, London*

Figure 110. Perfume bottle for Le Lys, fragrance by D'Orsay, molded R. LALIQUE, height 6½ in. (17 cm.).

Bottles of this type were relatively inexpensive to manufacture and made in large quantities, sometimes decorated with a colored *patine* as in this example. This model was made in three sizes and is usually marked with the name of the perfume on the stopper.

## Perfume Bottles, Garnitures de Toilette, and Glass Jewelry

By the mid-1920s it was impossible to imagine an elegant woman without perfume. The use of decorative containers and packaging in the perfume industry, which had been pioneered by Lalique and Coty before

Figure 109. The magnificent Fontaine des Parfums in the parfumerie section of the Paris Exposition of 1925, designed by Raguenet and Maillard with sculpture by Binet.

Most of the perfume bottles in this illustration are by René Lalique. Reprinted from *Devantures, Vitrines: Installations de Magazins à L'Exposition*, by René Herbst, 1925. Courtesy of Maison Gerard, New York

Figure 111. Powder box for D'Orsay with red patine, early 1920s, molded R. LALIQUE FRANCE, diameter 4 in. (10 cm.).

This model was manufactured as a production design by Lalique, without the molded lettering, entitled "Emiliane" (Design No. 70). Another version of the base was molded with flower heads.

Figure 112. A group of colored glass containers for Worth fragrances, 1920s.

The large bottle in the center was intended for display purposes; the spherical vessel on the left is a powder box modeled on the design of a popular perfume bottle which held the fragrances Dans la Nuit and Je Reviens. *Crystal Galleries*

Figure 113. "Fleurs Concave" perfume bottle, early 1920s, engraved R. Lalique, height 8½ in. (12 cm.).

This large bottle was sold without contents and intended to hold perfume or eau de toilette. *Gallerie Moderne*

Figure 114. Perfume bottle of wheat-sheaf form, in clear glass with blue enamel detailing, mid-1920s, molded R. LALIQUE MADE IN FRANCE, height 3¼ in. (8 cm.).

Enameling by hand was a feature of Lalique's glass which was rarely copied by his imitators. This unusual bottle retains its original amber-colored contents, identified by a paper label as the fragrance La Violette de Gabilla. *Collection of A. J. Tobias*

the war, acquired a new importance, largely due to the demands of foreign markets. The trends of the industry were outlined in the comprehensive general report on the Paris Exposition, published in September 1925:

> The taste for perfume has spread throughout every social class. Decorative bottles and boxes are no longer found exclusively in de luxe shops; they can be seen in innumerable storefronts in Paris and the provinces and appear in the most modest households. Designs by French artists are everywhere, at home and abroad, where the perfume industry is but a vehicle to aid the spread of French taste.[21]

The commercial significance of perfume bottle designs was evidenced by the scrutiny with which they were chosen. For example, in 1926, the House of Houbigant organized a design competition for a new flacon. Under the auspices of the Société d'Encouragement à l'Art et à l'Industrie, the competition drew more than 700 entries, which were judged by a distinguished panel, including Jean Puiforcat, Gerard Sandoz, and René Lalique.

*Figure 115. Perfume bottle in clear glass with black enamel detailing, mid-1920s, molded R. LALIQUE MADE IN FRANCE, engraved 287, height 3½ in. (8.4 cm.).*

Many of Lalique's perfume bottle designs, including this example, were sold without contents, to be used as decorative flacons at the dressing table. Bottles of this type were sold throughout Lalique's retail network and ranged from elaborate and expensive models to simpler designs such as this one.

As the undisputed master of perfume bottle design, Lalique produced an uninterrupted stream of flacons during the 1920s, creating 150 designs for at least a dozen *parfumeurs*, including Molinard, Houbigant, Coty, D'Orsay (Figures 110 and 111), Roger et Gallet, and the House of Worth (Figure 112).

The largest of Lalique's perfume bottle commissions was from Worth, which marketed its products on an unprecedented scale. The majority of Lalique's designs for Worth were of simple form and construction, and could be manufactured inexpensively in large quantities. In a measure to reduce costs, Worth bottles were rarely marked with the name of the fragrance, which was added to the stopper, allowing duplicate bottles to contain a variety of perfumes. As a further economy, stoppering by hand was discontinued for many Worth designs, especially after 1930.

Most of Lalique's commercial perfume bottles are marked with a molded signature, though a few exam-

*Figure 116. Lalique's designs for Le Jade fragrance by Roger et Gallet: powder box with contents and a perfume bottle, mid-1920s, height of bottle 3¼ in. (8.4 cm.).*

Handmade cardboard containers for cosmetics were introduced by François Coty before 1910 and used by numerous *parfumeurs* in the 1920s; this example was designed by René Lalique. The bottle is modeled like a Chinese snuff bottle and made in jade-green glass to emphasize the precious nature of its contents. *Weinstein Collection*

*Figure 117. Perfume bottle for No. 7, fragrance by Morabito, mid-1920s, height 5½ in. (14 cm.).*

Some of Lalique's finest perfume bottles were designed in the mid-1920s. This model, in cased, butterscotch-colored glass, is of exceptionally high quality. The Morabito No. 7 bottle was made in three sizes: 4½ in. (11.5 cm.), 5½ in. (14 cm.), and 8¼ in. (21.5 cm.). *Crystal Galleries*

ples are unmarked. Bottles intended for dressing table use and sold without contents are marked with either a molded signature or a more elaborate engraved script signature, or sometimes with both.

The success of the 1925 Exposition created demand for perfumes far beyond the dreams of François Coty and, coupled with Lalique's achievements, led to a flood of Lalique-style bottles and glassware of inferior quality. Within a few years, the shop windows of hairdressers and pharmacists throughout France were crammed with what Miguel Zamacoïs referred to as "blatant forgeries and cynically improvised imitations" [22] of Lalique's perfume bottle designs. Lalique expressed his indignation at those who would imitate him by stating:

Let them imitate my glass if they like. I will then throw up glass as I once threw up goldsmith's work. I will work in some other medium, in anything—in India rubber if you will! [23]

*Figure 118. Perfume bottles for a modern age, late 1920s.*

The bottle and atomizer in orange glass were designed to hold Worth fragrances. *Weinstein Collection*

Figure 119. Perfume atomizer for Molinard fragrances, late 1920s, height 3½ in. (8.5 cm.).

Several of Lalique's perfume bottle designs were also sold as atomizers. This model operates by a simple compression system; other examples were fitted with a squeeze bulb.

Lalique's response to his imitators was not as drastic as he had warned (although he did work briefly in the newly introduced material celluloid in 1925 and 1926). Rather, in characteristic fashion, he chose to discourage forgeries by improving the quality of his more expensive containers (which were most frequently copied), including the standards of molding, color, hand-applied work, and overall design. Thus, the presence of imitators presented a challenge to him which he met by designing some of the most lavish and extraordinary perfume bottles in the history of decorative art (Figures 114 and 117).

By the mid-1920s, "Madame" was able to fully equip her dressing table with Lalique accessories, in-

cluding boxes for powder, pommade, and trinkets, perfume and eau de cologne bottles, atomizers (Figure 119), mirrors (Figure 122), and picture frames (Figure 124). Lalique also manufactured three jewelry boxes in hardwoods set with decorative glass panels, patterned with butterflies, chrysanthemums or *monnaie du pape* leaves.

Figure 126 illustrates a selection of glass jewelry, the earliest examples of which were made at the

Figure 120. Perfume burner in frosted glass, late 1920s, molded R. LALIQUE, height 6 in. (15 cm.). Crystal Galleries

Figure 121. "Houppes" (Puffs) powder jar and cover, circa 1924, height 9 in. (23 cm.).

This charming design, termed a *grande boîte à poudre* by Lalique, was intended to hold powder puffs or cotton wool. The model was exhibited at the Paris Exposition in 1925. *Crystal Galleries*

made in this technique were manufactured into the 1930s and most are marked with a stamp in the metal backing.

Lalique's clear, colored, and opalescent glass jewelry was novel, attractive, and moderately priced, and achieved immediate popularity with the "flapper"

Figure 122. Toilet mirror in clear glass, late 1920s, metal backing stamped LALIQUE, height 18 in. (46 cm.).

This magnificent mirror is evidence that the quality of Lalique's glass was in no way jeopardized by the mass production of *garnitures de toilette. Collection of Mary Lou Utt*

Combs-la-Ville Glassworks before World War I. By the early 1920s Lalique was manufacturing a wide range of glass jewelry, including necklaces, bracelets, buckles, buttons, and pins and brooches with metal mounts. The majority of metal-mounted jewelry is made of clear glass and derives its iridescent, colorful sheen from light-reflecting metal foil "trapped" between the glass and mount. Brooches and bar pins

Figure 123. "Epines" (Thorns) wall mirror in clear, foil-backed glass with silvered brass terminals, diameter 17 in. (43 cm.).

René Lalique was not content to have his designs adorning dressing tables and boudoirs. By the mid-1920s Lalique glass could be found in the dining rooms, drawing rooms, and sitting rooms of fashionable households as his ideals of designing for *le hôme* were realized. Zamacoïs understood the reasons for Lalique's remarkable success, and recorded them in 1928:

Figure 124. "Lys" (Lilies) glass frame, circa 1928, height 8½ in. (22 cm.).

Frames of this type, intended for dressing table use, were available with clear glass panes or as mirrors, as in this example, which reflects the perfume bottle "Muguet." *Crystal Galleries*

generation. Necklaces and bracelets ranged in design from florid, Art Nouveau-inspired patterns to starkly geometric motifs. Pendants were pressed in a variety of shapes, often of Japanese *tsuba* form. Among the more expensive items were a small number of exquisite beaded necklaces in clear and frosted glass, resembling rock crystal, introduced during the late 1920s (Figure 125).

Lalique's all-glass jewelry is often unmarked, although pendants and larger pieces may be engraved with a script signature, sometimes without an initial "R."

*Figure 125. Necklace with bird design in clear and frosted glass beads, circa 1929.*

This sophisticated design was the "top of the line" of Lalique's glass jewelry in the late 1920s and cost more than many of the large colored vases. This example is contained in its original presentation box from the Place Vendôme showroom. *Collection of Mr. and Mrs. V. James Cole*

> One of [René Lalique's] greatest merits is his determination not to create objects purely for the sake of their beauty, but to enhance the beauty of all the objects with which we surround ourselves, bringing delight and renewed attractiveness to our everyday existence.[24]

Among the everyday objects to which Lalique applied his art was the ashtray, which acquired a new

*Figure 126. A selection of glass jewelry with metal mounts, circa 1913–1925.*

The green glass tripartite brooch was probably made at the Combs-la-Ville Glassworks before 1914. The three bar pins are in clear glass, colored by reflected light from metal foil trapped between the glass and mount. The set of buttons, with coiled serpent motif, is extremely rare. *Crystal Galleries*

*Figure 127. A selection of colored glass jewelry, 1920s.*

Lalique combined his extraordinary talents as a jeweler and experience as a glassmaker in his glass jewelry designs, which were remarkably diverse and superbly executed. *Crystal Galleries*

importance and demand in the liberated postwar society. Large numbers of women began to smoke for the first time in the Roaring Twenties and Lalique supplied them with elegant ash receivers in a spectrum of appealing colors (Figure 130).

Lalique continued to design writing desk accessories in the 1920s and many of his prewar models remained in production. Inkwells were normally of simple, circular form with a central covered well (Figure 128), or of a more elaborate, standish type, with pen-tray base fitted with wells, pounce jars, and letter seals. Seals were manufactured in both of Lalique's factories, with new designs being made at Wingen.

Figure 128. "Myrtilles" (Bilberries) inkwell in frosted glass with black enamel detailing, circa 1924 (Design No. 436), molded R. LALIQUE, diameter 8¼ in. (21 cm.).

The majority of Lalique's inkwells are of circular form with central covered well and are normally quite small, unlike this rare model, which is of large size.

Figure 129. "Double Marguerite" paperweight in red glass, circa 1922, wheel-cut R. LALIQUE, height 3 in. (8 cm.).

This model was also made as a seal in a smaller size.

Figure 130. A selection of ashtrays in colored glass, late 1920s.

René Lalique designed more than forty models of ashtrays during the 1920s, many of them composed of figural seals mounted on simple dish bases. *Crystal Galleries*

Figure 131. "Antilope" paperweight and "Caravelle" ashtray, late 1920s, heights 3¼ in. (8.2 cm.) and 3½ in. (9 cm.).

Many of Lalique's paperweights are functionally inadequate and were intended as decorative objects only.

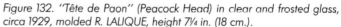

Figure 132. "Tête de Paon" (Peacock Head) in clear and frosted glass, circa 1929, molded R. LALIQUE, height 7¼ in. (18 cm.).

This model was offered as a paperweight (unmounted), an automobile mascot (with metal mount), and a bookend (mounted on black glass base as pictured).

Figure 133. Pair of "Tête de Coq" figures in clear and frosted glass, circa 1928, molded LALIQUE FRANCE, mounted as bookends on black glass bases.

Bases of this type are often mistaken for later mountings but they were added by the Lalique Company during the 1930s and a few examples are marked. The book in this photograph is a 1910 edition of Chantecler, a four-act play by Edmond Rostand, with an embossed leather cover designed by René Lalique. Crystal Galleries

The majority were in clear glass and most are of figural type.

Lalique's most commercially successful desktop accessory of the 1920s was the paperweight, of which more than forty models were put into production between 1925 and 1930 (Figure 129). Many of them were in the form of statuettes or models of birds, animals,

Figure 135. "Coq Houdan" mantel clock in clear and frosted glass, circa 1930, height 8 in. (20 cm.).

*Figure 134. Pair of "Coq Houdan" bookends in clear and frosted glass, circa 1930, wheel-cut R. LALIQUE, height 8 in. (20 cm.).*

The "Coq Houdan" model was also offered as a paperweight, an automobile mascot, and used to decorate a mantel clock (Figure 135). Crystal Galleries

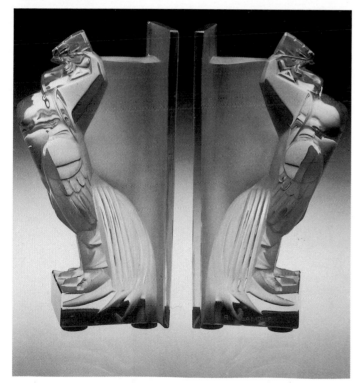

or insects, and were offered for sale under a variety of categories, including automobile mascots and bookends. This policy of multipurpose designs was frequently employed by Lalique, and helped to increase his range of ware, and thus his sales, while keeping production overhead to a minimum. Some "paperweight" figures were bolted on to black glass bases for use as bookends (Figures 132 and 133), and others were simplified or modified for the function (Figure 134). The "Coq Houdan" figure was also incorporated into the design of an extraordinary mantel clock (Figure 135).

Lalique designed more than twenty glass clocks during the 1920s, from tiny desk clocks (Figures 136 and 137) to decorative table clocks (Figure 138) and mantel clocks of impressive proportions (Figure 139). Small clocks were normally fitted with winding movements of Swiss manufacture of a type commonly used then. Larger clocks contained battery- or house-operated electric movements, most of which bear the mark of the manufacturer ATO. The majority of Lalique's clocks were made in clear or opalescent glass, and colored examples are extremely rare.

*Figure 136. "6 Hirondelles" (Swallows) clock in frosted glass, designed circa 1926, molded R. LALIQUE, height 6 in. (15 cm.).*

Small clocks of this type were intended for desk or dressing table use.

*Figure 137. Two of Lalique's pendulettes from the late 1920s, height of the taller 6 in. (15 cm.). Crystal Galleries*

## Automobile Mascots and La Vie au Dehors

Perhaps the Lalique Company's most innovative product of the 1920s was the motoring mascot, or automobile hood ornament.

The automobile was a status symbol of great distinction, out of the financial reach of all but the most affluent of individuals. It was not uncommon for members of elegant French society to decorate their cars in the highest contemporary style, echoing the bourgeois antics of their prerevolutionary ancestors, a form of overindulgence frowned upon by most serious decorative arts critics. A small number of prestige automobiles were displayed at the 1925 Exposition, de-

*Figure 138. "Roitelets" (Wrens) clock in clear and frosted glass, circa 1929, stenciled R. LALIQUE, height 8 in. (20 cm.).*

Clocks of this proportion were intended for use as "table clocks," which were popular during the 1920s. This model has an 8-day wind-up movement.

spite the remonstrances of a number of groups who persuaded the governing committees to require that automobiles be displayed without wheels on the pretext that they were "decorative objects" and not "transportation." The interiors were fitted with silk *fauteuils*, crystal decanters, and sumptuous cabinet-work, executed by leading *ébénistes* including Maurice Dufrène and Jean Dunand.

In 1925, the banner year of the golden age of French motoring, René Lalique was commissioned to contribute to automobile decoration by designing a glass mascot for the Citroën Company. The use of mascots, or *bouchons de radiateur* (literally "radiator stoppers," as they were called by the company), was not uncom-

mon (the famous "Spirit of Ecstasy" which adorns Rolls-Royce automobiles was designed by Charles Sykes in 1911), but they were normally of chromium-plated metal and often nothing more than an image of the manufacturer's logo or trademark. Lalique's first mascot, entitled "Five Horses" (after the Cinq Cheveaux automobile for which it was designed), was followed by a series of more than twenty mascots designed in the next five years, which ranged in appearance from breathtakingly symbolic to whimsical and cute.

*Figure 139. "Le Jour et la Nuit" (Day and Night) mantel clock, circa 1930, wheel-cut R. LALIQUE FRANCE, height 14½ in. (37.5 cm.).*

This model was the largest and most expensive of Lalique's clocks. The light and dark shading of the allegorical figures is achieved by molding them in intaglio and relief respectively. *Weinstein Collection*

72

*Figure 140. Two versions of the popular mascot "Longchamps," molded R. LALIQUE FRANCE, height 6 in. (15.5 cm.).*

The more realistic model of "Longchamps" (named after the French racecourse) was designed in 1928 and replaced by the more up-to-date version (*right*) about 1930. A third, and less common, horse-head mascot, entitled "Epsom" (after the English track), is modeled in forward straining position. *Crystal Galleries*

*Figure 141. This advertisement from a May 1929 issue of Autocar illustrates the most common method of mounting a Lalique mascot.*

*Figure 142. "Comète" automobile mascot in clear glass, designed in 1925, wheel-cut R. LALIQUE FRANCE, length 7½ in. (19 cm.).*

The Comet was the second motoring mascot Lalique designed for commercial production and one of only a few models exclusively intended for this purpose. *Collection of Mr. and Mrs. V. James Cole*

The adverse reaction that many critics felt toward the combination of automobiles and decorative art was levied, somewhat unfairly, at Lalique's mascots, evident in this extract from the influential magazine *Art et Industrie* in 1928:

> And, on the radiator cap, an *objet d'art* in glass; destined to be smashed one day by a spanner! . . . We must get rid of all this junk, elegance for the *nouveaux riches*.[25]

Despite a certain amount of bad press, Lalique's mascots met with popular demand from the motoring public, especially in Britain, where they were available through Lalique's London agents, the Breves Galleries (Figure 141). The majority of mascots were sold simultaneously as paperweights, and were probably designed as such. Together with "Five Horses," the only models which appear to have been designed for exclusive use as mascots are "Victoire" (Figure 146), "Comète" (Figure 142), and "Small Dragonfly," which are all unstable in an unmounted state. Mascots were normally made in clear or "white" glass, and colored examples are rare (Figures 144 and 145), though opalescent glass or clear glass with an amethyst tint is occasionally encountered (Figure 146).

The most common method of mounting the ornament was to screw it onto a radiator cap, which was prominent on the majority of production models of automobiles in the late 1920s. Another method was to set the figure farther back by drilling a hole through the hood and bolting the metal mount in place. Once in place, mascots could be lit in a spectrum of colors by means of an interchangeable light filter (available in green, blue, mauve, or amber) incorporated into the metal mount between the glass figure and a bulb that supplied illumination (Figure 146). Bulbs were

Figure 143. "Archer" automobile mascot in clear and frosted glass, designed circa 1928, molded R. LALIQUE, wheel-cut FRANCE, overall height 7½ in. (19 cm.).

The intaglio-molded Archer figure evidences Lalique's early work as a medalist. This example, which once adorned a 1932 Chrysler, is in its original mount, which has been modified to accommodate a pair of wings. *Collection of Mr. and Mrs. V. James Cole*

often operated by a dynamo system, thus increasing the light intensity with the increased speed of the vehicle. The Lalique Company supplied their own mounts, at a small charge, but this responsibility was left up to the retailer in foreign countries. The Breves Galleries manufactured and patented their own mounts in plated brass, stamped with their address and patent information (Figure 146).

The most successful of Lalique's motoring mascot

Figure 144. "Coq Nain" (Dwarf Cockerel) and "Grande Libellule" (Large Dragonfly) automobile mascots in purple glass, late 1920s, molded R. LALIQUE FRANCE, heights 8¼ in. (20.5 cm.) and 8⅜ in. (21 cm.).

Automobile mascots were rarely made in colored glass. These examples are extremely rare. *Crystal Galleries*

Figure 145. "Perche" automobile mascot in opalescent yellow glass, designed circa 1928, wheel-cut R. LALIQUE FRANCE, length 7¼ in. (18 cm.).

René Lalique chose some extraordinary subjects for his automobile mascots, including a turkey, a wild boar, a frog, and this fish, which is very definitely "out-of-water."

designs is the model "Victoire" (Figure 146), also known as "Spirit of the Wind" in England and sometimes called "Seminole" in the United States. "Victoire," which is often referred to as the "Rolls-Royce mascot" because of its frequent use on expensive automobiles, is a superb design achievement, quite unlike anything Lalique had designed previously and

Figure 146. "Victoire" automobile mascot in amethyst-tinted clear glass, designed in 1925, molded R. LALIQUE FRANCE, with plated brass mount from Breves Galleries, length 10 in. (25.5 cm.).

In this photograph the mascot is illuminated by a clear bulb housed in the metal mount, giving the figure a magical appearance. Lalique captured the spirit of the age in "Victoire," which has become a symbol of the Art Deco period and a masterpiece of "le style Lalique." *Author's Collection*

Figure 147. *Commemorative statuette in frosted glass, 1929, wheel-cut R. LALIQUE, height 6½ in. (16.5 cm.).*

This model, which is often mistaken for an automobile mascot, was commissioned by the Compagnie des Wagons-Lits to commemorate the inauguration of their Côte d'Azur Pullman line in 1929.

wholly appropriate for its function. The model captures the spirit of the "age of speed," and it would be difficult for any contemporary critic to deny its merit as a symbol of inspiration.

The sport of motoring was part of an emerging culture known in France as *la vie au dehors.*[26] The "outdoor life" drew esthetes and other members of fashionable society to the splendid Côte d'Azur or the Alps in wintertime, and to the countryside in summer. The railroad companies enjoyed their last great period of prosperity and reequipped rolling stock in a style befitting the luxurious requirements of the wealthy traveler. At the 1925 Exposition a number of companies displayed their finest carriages, complete with freestanding *fauteuils*, luxurious carpets, ironwork, and

cabinetry by leading designers and *ébénistes*. One of the most successful was the Compagnie des Wagons-Lits, whose overnight lines included the famous North Star express between Paris and Amsterdam. In 1926 it organized a competition for the interior design of a new sleeping car to serve the Côte d'Azur, and chose a scheme using Lalique frosted glass panels, molded in shallow relief with grapevines and bacchanalian figures (Figure 148). Lalique had worked for the Compagnie des Wagons-Lits in 1923, designing panels which were incorporated into a presidential sleeping car. Unlike the presidential panels, those used on the Côte d'Azur line were a standard production model, designed before 1925, in which year they were available in the Place Vendôme showroom.[27] In addition to the wall panels, Lalique designed a statuette to commemorate the opening of the Cote d'Azur line in 1929 (Figure 147).

## Lighting and Illuminated Glass

René Lalique was described in 1927 as "that rarest of individuals, a practical man as well as a talented artist."[28] These two qualities were never more successfully combined than in the design of decorative lighting. The rapid spread of domestic electricity after the war led to an important new industry in lighting manufacture, which the Lalique Company spearheaded in France throughout the 1920s. René Lalique

Figure 148. *Panel in frosted glass with gray patine, before 1925, of a design used in the division walls of carriages on the Côte d'Azur Pullman line, opened by the Compagnie des Wagons-Lits in 1929.*

Rolling stock with this design was also used on the famous Orient Express in the 1930s. *Crystal Galleries*

This early table lamp is designed for an "age of elegance" and pre-dates the modernist style Lalique adopted in the mid-1920s. *Phillips, New York*

*Figure 150. "Cardamine" table lamp in clear and frosted glass with chromium-plated metal stand, circa 1928, engraved R. Lalique France, height 17½ in. (44.5 cm.).*

By the late 1920s Lalique's table lamp designs were boldly geometric and of stark, modernist outline, in contrast to the earlier "softer" designs (Figure 149). The electrical cords in this model are housed in two barely visible metal tubes attached to each side of the standard.

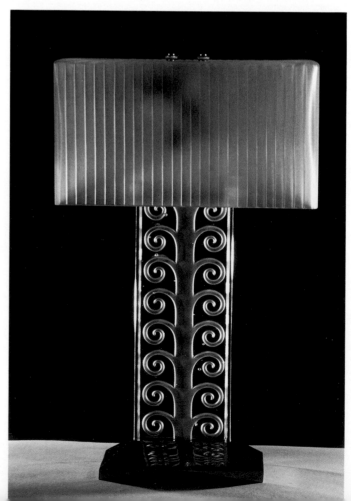

Figure 151. Pair of "Coquilles" (Shells) plafonniers *in opalescent glass,* *late 1920s, wheel-cut R. LALIQUE FRANCE and engraved No. 3201, di-* *ameter 8 in. (20 cm.).*

A number of Lalique's *plafonniers* were production bowls converted into lighting fixtures, including "Coquilles," which was made in two sizes, this being the smaller. The hardware on these examples, which was probably fitted by the Breves Galleries, allows the bowl to be used as a hanging fixture or, by using the ring mount, as a ceiling attachment or wall applique of bulkhead type.

exploited the advantage of a large, modern manufacturing facility by designing a vast range of lighting fixtures, and achieved supremacy over his closest competitors, including Maurice-Ernest Sabino, Genet et Michon, and Jean Perzel.

Table lamps were manufactured at the Wingen Glassworks from about 1921. The earliest designs were of traditional form with "organic" decoration, typical of Lalique's premodernism (Figure 149). He designed more than twenty-five table lamps during the interwar period, including at least one made in collaboration with the ironworker Edgar Brandt.[29] The

Figure 152. "Lampe Bague Personnages" *in frosted glass, circa 1922 (De-* *sign No. 2152), engraved R. Lalique France, height 18½ in. (46.5 cm.).*

This lamp, which was designed to provide indirect light, was made in three versions, identical except for the loose *bague,* or collar, which was available in a serpent or leaf design as well as this figural pattern. *Phillips, New York*

*Figure 153. Chandelier in frosted glass, circa 1928.*

Lalique's glass was ideally suited to diffuse light, creating a soft, warm radiance. This unwieldy design is one of Lalique's more bizarre creations and is stylistically akin to the work of several of his contemporaries, including Sabino. *Reprinted from* Le Luminaire *by Guillaume Janneau, 2nd Series (1928), pl. 29.*

*Figure 155. "Feuillage" (Leafage) applique in frosted glass with sepia patine, late 1920s, molded R. LALIQUE, length 13¼ in. (35.5 cm.).*

Lalique's simpler *appliques* were light bowls molded only as half-sections. Fixtures of this type were relatively inexpensive and widely used during the 1920s and 1930s. *Phillips, New York*

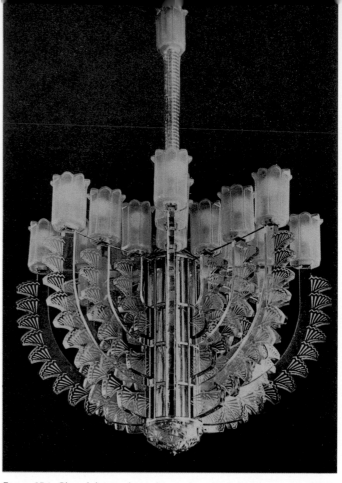

*Figure 154. Chandelier in clear glass with etched decoration, late 1920s.*

Chandeliers of this proportion were more commonly used by commercial patrons than private invididuals. Note the lamp shade used as a ceiling cap and the lengths of glass tubing which shield the hanging chain and cord. *Reprinted from* Le Luminaire, *by Guillaume Janneau, 2nd Series (1928), pl. 27.*

majority of table lamps were sold complete with glass shades, though some models were offered with silk shades as an option. Production vases were converted into lamps in France and England in the 1920s and 1930s. This was accomplished by fitting a metal bulb-mount into the neck of the vessel and hanging the cord on the outside. Lamps of this type were supplied with glass, silk, or mesh shades. Lalique vases that have been drilled and mounted as lamps were probably converted by private owners and not by the original retailer.

*Figure 156. The frontispiece of a brochure printed by the Breves Galleries of London in the late 1920s, featuring the most expensive model from an impressive range of light fixtures.*

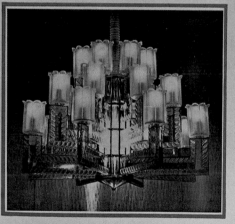

*Figure 157. "Grande Boule de Gui" (Mistletoe) hanging light fixture in clear and frosted glass with green patine, height 36 in. (90 cm.).*

Lalique displayed a wide variety of decorative lighting at the 1925 Exposition, including this fine example of "caged" lighting. *Gallerie Moderne*

By the mid-1920s, traditional methods of placing, hanging, and mounting lights were avoided by interior designers who discovered and explored the use of indirect lighting and concealed or "caged" light (Figure 157). Indirect light was normally derived from freestanding floor lamps, which Lalique did not design, although a few table lamps were designed for the purpose (Figure 152).

Lalique's hanging light fixtures fall into two general categories: *plafonniers*, or light bowls, which could either be hung or be attached directly to a ceiling (Figure 151), and *lustres*, or chandeliers. *Plafonniers* were normally manufactured in clear or opalescent glass, which reacts splendidly to transmitted light, and were often highlighted with *patine*. Colored examples are

Figure 158. "Oiseau de Feu" (Firebird) surtout with bronze illuminating stand, mid-1920s, molded R. LALIQUE, height 17¼ in. (43 cm.).

This mythical image was inspired by the *Firebird Symphony*, composed by Igor Stravinsky, which was performed in Paris during World War I by the Ballets Russes.

Figure 159. "3 Paons" (Peacocks) surtout with bronze illuminating stand, late 1920s, engraved R. Lalique, length 36 in. (91 cm.).

Surtouts were among the most expensive of Lalique's production ware, which accounts for their rarity today.

most commonly in a pale amber glass, although a deep orange color is occasionally encountered (Figure 183).

René Lalique designed about twenty-five models of *plafonniers* during the 1920s, some of which were in the form of converted table bowls. The most common method of hanging was by silken cords, with or without ceiling caps. A small additional charge was made for *attaches*, or complementary glass plaques, which were attached to the cords or used as links between the cord and bowl. Metal-link chains and other hardware were supplied by, and in some cases designed by, the retailer in Lalique's foreign outlets.

*Plafonniers* were often accompanied by matching *appliques*, or wall fixtures, which were especially popular in traditional interior design. Lalique produced about thirty models of *applique* during the 1920s, many of which were simply *plafonniers* of half-sections (Figure 155), fitted with metal mounts and backplate. Lalique's range of wall fixtures ranged from simple bowls to elaborate sconces of floral or vase form. A few *appliques* were of *surtout* type, consisting of plaques molded with various designs in intaglio, illuminated from beneath from metal mounts.

The avoidance of hanging fixtures led to the intro-

*Figure 160. Two "tiara" luminaires molded with designs of carnations and roses, height 7 in. (17.5 cm.).*

Small lamps of this type were probably intended for boudoir use. The "stoppers" terminate in a central lug and rest loosely in the bases, which are of standard design. In all, five styles of base were manufactured for seven small luminaire designs. *Crystal Galleries*

duction of cornice lighting, pioneered in the 1920s by Genet et Michon. A unique form of cornice fixture was designed by René Lalique for use in new design or interior renovation.[30] The fixtures, glass panels of quarter-round sections with decorative molding on the convex exterior, enjoyed limited success, despite receiving overwhelming praise in 1926 from the influential art critic and great admirer of René Lalique, Gabriel Mourey:

> Lalique's latest creation is [the design of] glass cornices, to be placed at the top of ordinary plaster walls

in order to conceal the terrible plaster cornices which unfortunately one nearly always sees there. They are molded in lengths of about three feet which fit together with great exactitude, and which, thanks to a special arrangement, can hold electric globes, thus throwing down into the room a diffused light of the utmost charm.[31]

Lalique designed five models of cornice light, patterned with grapevines, dahlias, hornbeam, thistles, and acacia, all of which were made in two lengths (1 meter and 56 cm.). The plaques were used in the interior design of the Cannes showroom for the House of Worth, completed in 1926, which included an Art Deco portico in illuminated frosted glass panels. The Worth showroom project was one of a number of commissions for architectural design and lighting which Lalique caried out. His other important projects included the design of lighting fixtures for the French passenger liner *Paris*, launched in 1920; the renovation of the fashionable Arcades des Champs-Elysées, completed in 1926, which included four large exterior lamps and fifty interior lights, as well as an illuminated fountain; and the light fixtures for the infamous Paris nightclub Le Lido (where aquatic spectacles were performed in an enormous swimming pool), completed in 1929.

René Lalique completed two important architectural commissions in the United States in the 1920s: the design of the lobby interior, including entrance doors, elevator doors, vitrines, and an illuminated ceiling, for the Alexander and Oviatt department store in the Oviatt Building in Los Angeles, which was completed in 1927, and, in the following year, the designs of the "crystal room" and entrance salon for the Jay Thorpe Building in New York.

All of Lalique's lighting fixtures were designed to diffuse and project light through the glass, exploiting the translucent properties of the material and creating a soft, warm radiance. Thus, Lalique's *lustres* were fundamentally different from traditional chandeliers, which rely on the brilliance of facet-cut glass to reflect a maximum amount of light. Designs for *lustres* ranged from the traditional (Figure 154) to the entirely unconventional (Figure 153) and bizarre. Larger chandeliers were most commonly used by commercial patrons (in the interiors of hotels and department stores, for example), including the Alexander and Oviatt store, where Lalique chandeliers hung in the exclusive *salon des élégantes* on the main floor.

Many of the branched chandeliers were fitted with *tulipes*, or lamp shades, which were made in three different designs and occasionally used as ceiling caps (Figure 154). Hanging chains and electrical cords were concealed with glass *motifs d'accrochage*, which were simply lengths of glass tube, made in spiraled or grooved patterns (Figure 154). Smaller hanging wires were concealed within lengths of clear glass piping of plain design.

About 1925, Lalique began to manufacture a range of glass and metal *surtouts*, or decorative illuminated plaques which are sometimes referred to as "luminaires." Lalique's *surtouts* were impractical as lighting devices, an aspect of their design which drew some unfavorable comments from critics who had admired

*Figure 161. "Inséparables" (Lovebirds) luminaire in clear and frosted glass, late 1920s, height 17 in. (42.5 cm.)*

Luminaires of this type were mainly used as decorative objects as they gave little light and were relatively fragile. *Crystal Galleries*

Lalique's impeccable combination of form and function in design. Most *surtouts* are in the form of glass plates, up to two inches in thickness, molded with complex intaglio designs highlighted with frosting against a clear, polished ground (Figures 158 and 159). The plaques, which derive light from beneath through incandescent bulbs housed in the metal bases, display the luminescent qualities of Lalique's glass to maximum effect. Lalique designed sixteen illuminated *surtouts* in the 1920s, the largest and most expensive of which were two arc-shaped plaques of horizontal emphasis, which were the company's highest-priced production designs, exclusive of a few chandeliers. The plaques depict three peacocks (Figure 159), and two mythical knights in armor ("Deux Cavaliers"), and are mounted on bronze bases patterned with briars and ivy leaves respectively.

Surtouts are usually marked with an engraved or wheel-cut signature, though some examples are signed in the mold. Bronze bases are sometimes stamped LALIQUE, and plated metal bases are unsigned.

René Lalique combined the luminescent qualities of his glass *surtouts* with the commercial success of table lamps in a range of "tiara" luminaires designed in the late 1920s. The luminaires can be considered decorative objects as they give little light and are quite fragile and unwieldy. The tiara concept was derived from a perfume bottle design, introduced by Lalique before the war (Figures 20 and 23), and luminaires of this type were presumably intended for boudoir or dressing table usage (Figure 160). The tiara series included four designs of impressive proportions, all of which shared a ribbed, bottle-form base (Figure 161).

## Table Glass

Most of Lalique's commercial production during the 1920s was in the form of functional table glass. The range of ware contained every conceivable object for the fashionable host or hostess, each one made in a multiplicity of designs. René Lalique had designed and manufactured drinking glasses since 1905,[32] but he did not enter the realm of large-scale table glass manufacture until after 1925, by which time the company's retail empire had greatly expanded and a sufficient demand existed for successful commercial

*Figure 162. Carafe and wineglasses in the "Strasbourg" pattern, circa 1925, height of decanter 10 in. (25.5 cm.).*

This pattern of glassware was exhibited by Lalique at the 1925 Exposition. Complete sets of table glass, including four sizes of drinking vessel, finger bowls, and plates of various sizes, were available in the "Strasbourg" pattern and other popular designs. *William Christie Collection*

Figure 163. "Frise Personnages" and "Chasse-Chiens," two drinking goblets with sepia patine, 1920s, height 6 in. (14.5 cm.) and 5½ in. (13 cm.). Weinstein Collection

production. Traditionally, table glass was in the form of brilliantly cut crystal, appraised more on the prestige of its manufacturer than on its decorative merit. Lalique's molded ware met with immediate public approval, despite the deviation from tradition, and has remained popular ever since.

Lalique's full, or *grande ceremonie*, table services consisted of a decanter, water goblet, three sizes of wineglass, and a champagne goblet. Smaller (*demi-ceremonie*) services were also available. The majority of drinking glasses have traditionally shaped bowls, with decoration limited to the stems and stoppers of de-

canters. In the 1920s, however, a new, goblet form of drinking vessel was introduced, and described in the interior design magazine *Good Furniture and Decoration* in 1929:

> [Lalique's] goblet group may be either straight or almost cylindrical for the part holding the liquid, or it may bulge in different ways. However, in all cases there must be a good balance of volume and the cen-

Figure 164. Liquor carafe designed for the wine merchant Cusenier, circa 1925.

Cusenier was the François Coty of the wine and spirits trade in the 1920s. He commissioned *flaçons d'art* from René Lalique, Raoul Lachenal, and René Herbst for his products, which were sold throughout Europe and in South America. Reprinted from *La Musée de la Double Soif* by Edmond Haraucourt (ed. Cusenier), 1925. *Photo: The Corning Museum of Glass, Corning, New York*

*Figure 165. "Masques" carafe with sepia patine, designed circa 1912, engraved R. Lalique France, height 10½ in. (27 cm.).*

Lalique manufactured individual decanters of high quality as well as table service carafes. "Masques" is one the earliest carafe designs and was available with three stoppers, including the mushroom-shaped example shown, which was used from about 1930. Collection of Robert and Karen Ettinger

ter of gravity must be placed as near to the table as possible. This is especially true for glasses intended for use on dining cars or steamships.[33]

Lalique's goblet groups are well balanced and extremely practical without any sacrifice in elegance of line (Figure 163). In the 1930s René Lalique did in-

deed design table glass for a French steamship company, the Compagnie Général Transatlantique, which operated the famous liner *Normandie*, and he appears to have followed the critics' advice in the design for drinking glasses, which are of a short-stemmed type, resembling eggcups in outline.

The CGT stemware was not the first commercial commission Lalique received for table glass. In 1924 he designed two models of carafe for the wine merchant Cusenier, which were exhibited in Cusenier's display at the Paris Exposition of 1925.[34] Cusenier was a great entrepreneur with a network of retail stores throughout France and Belgium and in Buenos Aires. Like François Coty he understood the importance of packaging his wares and, like Coty, he commissioned René Lalique to provide the finest containers for his products. Lalique's two carafe designs for Cusenier were of identical form (termed *forme Cusenier* by the Lalique Company),[35] molded with handles in a bramble pattern (Figure 164), and of satyr design. The satyr model, known as "Carafe Faune," was put into production and retailed by Lalique (Design No. 3167), but production pieces are distinguishable from Cusenier's commissions, which are engraved with his name on the base. Cusenier preserved a remarkable collection of oenophilia in a private museum, humorously called La Musée de la Double Soif, which was recorded in a catalogue by Edmond Haraucourt in 1925.[36]

In addition to wine-related glass, Lalique manufactured a wide range of tableware, including plates for salad and dessert, bowls of every description, water jugs, tumblers, liquor decanters (Figure 165), and cheese plates. Cocktail sets were popular during the 1920s and Lalique supplied a number of designs, some including shakers in the form of ingeniously converted small production vases. Glass swizzle sticks were a rather fragile extra, available in boxed sets of twelve. Orangeade and soft drink services were made, usually in bright orange glass, complete with trays to facilitate serving outdoors (Figure 166).

Lalique's enormous range of decorative table accessories included candlesticks (Figures 167 and 168),

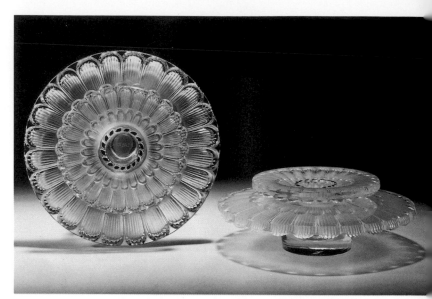

*Figure 166. Orangeade service in the "Bahia" pattern, late 1920s, stenciled R. LALIQUE FRANCE, diameter of tray 16½ in. (42 cm.).*

René Lalique designed five soft-drink services which were made in clear or orange glass. A complete service comprises a tray, jug, and six glasses. *Weinstein Collection*

*Figure 167. A pair of "Dahlia" pattern candlesticks with black enamel "stamens," circa 1925, stenciled R. LALIQUE, diameter 5½ in. (14.5 cm.).*

The upper *bobèche* of the "Dahlia" candlestick is removable to allow a single example to serve as two sticks.

menu and place card holders (Figure 169), knife rests, ashtrays, pepper mills, condiment sets, and individual cigarette jars (Figure 170).

Together with functional objects, Lalique designed a variety of purely ornamental table decorations, mostly of figural type. The first of these *garnitures de table* were displayed at exhibitions, including the Paris Exposition of 1925, and included a footed statuette entitled "Caryatid," of identical form to the "Figurine" candlestick illustrated in Figure 168, but minus the candle nozzle. In the late 1920s Lalique introduced his enormously successful bird models, which were originally intended as table decorations. The placement of figural ornaments on banquet tables was a

European tradition rooted in the early eighteenth century, when figurines were modeled in silver or porcelain. Lalique's designs revived this practice briefly during the interwar period, and the bird models have remained among the company's most popular products ever since.

Service plates have traditionally displayed the decorative art and taste of the society for which they were manufactured. Prior to the 1920s, glass plates were usually plain or pressed in traditional "cut-glass" patterns. René Lalique transformed the glass plate into an object of beauty and refinement, and it is unlikely that, in the history of decorative art, any other individual has been responsible for such a myriad of plate designs (Figures 171, 172, 173, and 175).

Plates and shallow bowls were cheap and easy to manufacture by a single pressing, and required little hand finishing or decoration. The great majority of Lalique's plate designs are of symmetrical or radiating pattern, molded in shallow, undulating relief on the verso to increase the luminescent effect of the opales-

*Figure 168. Three pairs of table candlesticks, including (left to right) "Figurine" (Design No. 2103), "St. James" (No. 2126), and an anonymous pair, mid-1920s.*

Despite the popularity of Lalique's table glass, candlesticks in silver or cut crystal were preferred on many fashionable tables during the 1920s and Lalique examples are quite rare. *Crystal Galleries*

Figure 169. A selection of menu and place card holders in clear and frosted glass, circa 1924–1930.

Lalique's table accessories were often wittily and exquisitely designed. At least four models of large menu card holder were manufactured and up to a dozen of the smaller type are recorded. *Crystal Galleries*

cent glass, which was most commonly used in plate manufacture. Plates and shallow bowls were suitable for display when not in use, especially the larger, heavier models which were principally intended for this purpose (Figure 174).

Deeper bowls, called *coupes*, were manufactured in a wide variety of designs, including several with matching plate patterns. *Coupes* were normally used to hold fruit or salad, and some models were available with straight or incurved walls to differentiate between these two uses. Plates, shallow bowls, and coupes were normally marked with a molded signature (especially those designs made in the 1930s), which is sometimes hidden in the pattern. Wheel-cut signatures were used on larger models and a few bowls, including the popular "Coquilles" series, and stenciled signatures were also common then. Between 1921 and about 1925 some designs of bowl made at the Wingen Glassworks in Alsace were marked with a raised VDA monogram in a square border. The monogram, standing for Verrerie d'Alsace (Alsace Glass-

Figure 171. Plate in opalescent glass, circa 1928, stenciled R. LALIQUE FRANCE, diameter 14 in. (36 cm.).

The wheat ear was one of René Lalique's favorite design motifs, which he first used on glass about 1900.

Figure 172. Shallow bowl in opalescent glass, late 1920s, molded R. LALIQUE, diameter 11½ in. (29.5 cm.).

Serving plates were extremely popular due to their impressive appearance and relatively low retail price. This example is highly suitable for serving cold fish or seafood hors d'oeuvres.

Figure 170. Pair of individual cigarette jars in the "Lierre" (Ivy) pattern with sepia patine, circa 1925 (Design No. 1121), height 3 in. (7.8 cm.).

*Porte cigarettes* were popular during the 1920s, when heavy smoking was common in fashionable social circles. Today they are often mistaken for shot glasses. *Crystal Galleries*

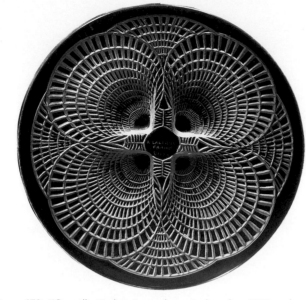

*Figure 173. "Coquilles" plate in opalescent glass, late 1920s, wheel-cut R. LALIQUE FRANCE, engraved No. 3103, diameter 6½ in. (16.2 cm.).*

The pattern of overlapping shells appears on a range of plates and bowls made in five different sizes, some of which were also used as hanging light fixtures (Figure 151).

*Figure 175. Shallow bowl in opalescent glass, late 1920s, engraved R. Lalique France, diameter 11¼ in. (28.5 cm.).*

In this striking design the peacock "eyes" are modeled as protruding, cabochon forms, giving them a jewellike quality in transmitted light.

*Figure 174. "Martigues" shallow bowl in opalescent amber glass, circa 1926, molded R. LALIQUE, diameter 14¼ in. (36.5 cm.).*

Bowls of this type, normally made in opalescent or colored glass, were principally designed as decorative objects. *Bonhams, London*

*Figure 176. "Perruches" (Parakeets) bowl in pale green opalescent glass, late 1920s, stenciled R. LALIQUE FRANCE, diameter 10 in. (25.5 cm.).*

This model of *coupe* was extremely popular during the 1930s, especially in England. It was normally made in clear or opalescent glass and the pale green variety is quite rare. *Collection of A. J. Tobias*

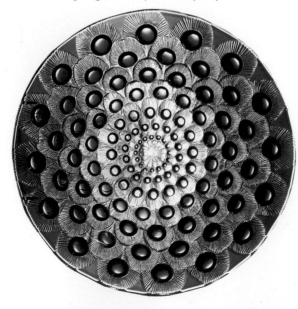

Figure 177. *"Cléones"* (Beetles) bonbonnière *in amber glass, early 1920s, molded R. LALIQUE, diameter 6½ in. (17 cm.).*

Boxes of this size, with glass bases, were intended to hold sweetmeats. They were usually made in opalescent glass and colored examples are uncommon.

works), commemorated the opening of the new factory, an event the company used to generate publicity and prestige.

Jardinières and *bonbonnières* are included in the Table Glass section of this book as they were intended for use on tables or to adorn sideboards in dining rooms (Figure 178). Lalique designed more than a dozen *jardinières* during the 1920s, including a small, star-shaped example called "Etoile," which is frequently mistaken for an oversized ashtray.

Figure 178. *"Saint Hubert"* jardinière *in clear and frosted glass, mid-1920s, wheel-cut R. LALIQUE FRANCE, length 18½ in. (47 cm.).*

# 4. "LE STYLE LALIQUE": THE EVOLUTION OF A STYLE

Together with imagination, which is the most magnificent gift that nature can bestow on an artist, the principal qualities of René Lalique are taste and conscience.[1]

Miguel Zamacoïs's observation in 1928 is an accurate description of the ingredients in Lalique's design genius. Even in his writings, however, Zamacoïs, who was Lalique's great personal friend, gave little indication of how he combined these ingredients to formulate his unique conceptual vision.

René Lalique was a private individual, naturally shy, and intentionally discreet in discussing the philosophical or practical aspects of his work. In a rare, published interview during the Paris Exposition of 1925, Lalique was asked by the art critic Maximilian Gauthier to define the methods and principles he followed in the execution of his work. Lalique's response is a graphic disclosure of his design process, which he referred to as a "perpetual task":

> I look at, I examine; a woman, a child, a bird in flight, whatever; a tree alive in the sunlight appears as a fish beneath the water; suddenly, the harmony of a shape, a gesture, a movement, becomes locked in my mind, combining with other ideas I have already acquired. Only when I have turned it all over and over in my head, does the idea, the *oeuvre*, ripen, and only then do I harvest it.[2]

Much of Lalique's success can be attributed to this accumulative design process, whereby he was constantly "turning over" new ideas, each one inspired or enhanced to some degree by earlier work or experience. The process was identified early in Lalique's glassmaking career in this extract from a review of the Lalique exhibition at Agnew's Gallery, London, in 1905:

> There is in [Lalique's] work, suggestions of the past to be easily discovered, and yet originality in every one of his designs.[3]

It is the originality that, when isolated, can be considered Lalique's design genius. Although he made extensive and repetitive use of traditional decorative images and motifs, Lalique was an innovator, never a renovator, and his artistry displays a sense of balance and control rarely found outside the fine arts. The "suggestions of the past" which appear in Lalique's work are drawn from the stimulating environments of his youth and early career, which overflowed with a staggering variety of images, styles, and esthetic philosophies on which Lalique feasted his remarkable powers of observation and artistic interpretation.

Lalique acquired a love of the natural world from the pastoral surroundings of his birthplace in Champagne, the home of his mother's family, where he spent summers during childhood, and from the woodlands around his estate at Clairfontaine. During his formative years in Paris, Lalique was exposed to the sumptuous neobaroque style of the French Second Empire, best exemplified in the opulent Paris Opera Building, completed when Lalique was fifteen years old. Neoclassicism was also strongly evident in the Paris of Lalique's youth, and collections of Greek, Roman, and Egyptian sculpture and artifacts dominated the Musée du Louvre. The traditional styles were usurped somewhat during the third quarter of the nineteenth century by the introduction of Japanese art into Europe and the ensuing taste for Japonisme, which made a strong impact on Lalique, intensified during his period of association with Samuel Bing, the greatest promoter of the Japanese style in French decorative arts.

When René Lalique began to study sculpture, in 1880, the popular sculptors were of the previous generation and included Albert Ernest Carrier-Belleuse (1824–1887) and Jean-Baptiste Carpeaux (1827–1875), who worked in a "decorative" revivalist style, loosely in the manner of Clodion. René Lalique adopted the graceful poses and smooth outlines of their work for his figural designs in glass, notably the tiny figurine stoppers he designed for perfume bottles and *garnitures de toilette* (Figures 179 and 181). Like his contemporary Auguste Rodin (who had apprenticed under Carrier-Belleuse), Lalique interpreted the style to a degree where it became his own. "Le style Lali-

que" is perhaps best identified in the vase "Bacchantes" (Figure 180), Lalique's most celebrated and best-known design, which demonstrates his remarkable abilities as a sculptor and understanding of the vital properties of translucent glass. The vase is modeled in the form of an architectural frieze: the figures would "work" at any scale—indeed, their beauty would increase in proportion to their size.

Although Lalique worked briefly in the medieval style of the English arts and crafts movement (Figure

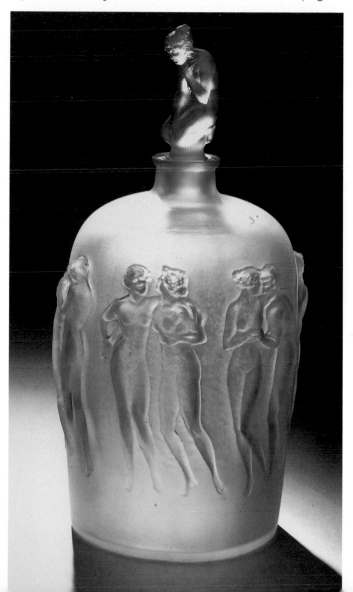

*Figure 179. Flask and stopper in frosted glass, circa 1924, engraved R. Lalique France No. 914, height 11¼ in. (28.8 cm.).*

This elegant vessel was intended as a decorative object or to hold eau de toilette. The manneristic modeling and sensuous quality of the figures is characteristic of Lalique's designs of the early 1920s. *Collection of Robert and Karen Ettinger*

*Figure 180. "Bacchantes" vase in yellow glass, stenciled R. LALIQUE FRANCE, height 9½ in. (25 cm.).*

This is one of René Lalique's most popular and successful designs; a version of the model is still manufactured in frosted glass. *Weinstein Collection*

*Figure 181. "Amphytrite" perfume bottle in green glass, circa 1922, molded R. LALIQUE, height 3½ in. (9.5 cm.).*

René Lalique adopted the smooth outlines and graceful poses preferred by 19th-century French sculptors in his modeling of figurines. The tiny stopper on this bottle is only one-half inch in height. *Crystal Galleries*

Figures 182 and 183, but all can be considered typical of "le style Lalique," illustrating the designer's versatility and adaptability. Quite different, but also typical and exemplary of Lalique's evolutionary style, is the vase "Danaïdes" (Figure 184), another vessel decorated with mythological female figures in relief. The daughters of Danaus are molded in low, flattened re-

*Figure 183. "Sirènes" plafonnier in opalescent orange glass, molded R. LALIQUE, diameter 15 in. (38.2 cm.).*

Following the opening of his first glassworks in 1909 Lalique developed a languid, half-mystical, half-sensuous style, using symbolistic images. The silver mounts on this early example of "Sirènes" are original.

*Figure 182. "Sirènes" perfume burner in opalescent glass, circa 1914, molded R. LALIQUE, height 7 in. (18 cm.).*

The classical modeling of the bacchantes in Figure 180 contrasts with the Art Nouveau-inspired style of the sirens Lalique depicted on a variety of glass objects during the 1920s, including this magnificent hanging lamp bowl, photographed to show the effect of transmitted light on the opalescent-colored glass. *Crystal Galleries*

12), he had abandoned it in favor of French taste before the opening of the Combs-la-Ville Glassworks in 1909. There Lalique developed a languid, half-mystical, half-sensuous, though rarely sensual, style, using symbolistic images and occasionally flirting with allegory (Figures 182, 183, and 39).

The classical modeling of the bacchantes in Figure 180 contrasts with the Art Nouveau-inspired sirens in

lief, partially clad and stylized in the Art Deco taste, favored at the time of design, around 1924. "Danaïdes" demonstrates the tendency for Lalique's post-1920 designs to become repeating or symmetrical, in contrast to the earlier, random style. The first evidence of this tendency toward symmetry appears in the immediate postwar period (Figure 185).

The same evolutionary pattern exists in Lalique's glass sculpture, the earliest examples of which are modeled in a symbolistic style, reminiscent of La

Figure 185. Vase in cire perdue glass, circa 1920, height 9¼ in. (23.5 cm.).

The arrangement of the two equestrians on this vessel is an early example of symmetry in decoration, which characterized Lalique's designs from about 1925. Calouste Gulbenkian Museum, Lisbon

Figure 186. "Grande Nue, Longue Cheveux" statuette in clear and frosted glass, on ebonized wood stand, engraved R. Lalique France No. 836, height 15½ in. (41 cm.).

The earliest of Lalique's sculptures are modeled in a symbolistic style, clearly inspired by the results of casting glass in the cire perdue technique. Bonhams, London

Figure 187. "Source de la Fontaine" statuette in frosted glass on laquered wood stand, circa 1924, wheel-cut R. LALIQUE FRANCE, height 22 in. (57 cm.).

By the mid-1920s Lalique's sculptural glass was modeled in the stylized manner of contemporary taste. Phillips, New York

Figure 188. "Madonna and Child" statuette in frosted glass with black glass base, circa 1950, engraved Lalique France, height 14½ in. (37 cm.).

This statuette was produced after 1945 and the design is attributed to Marc Lalique. The simplified modeling is a development from the geometric stylizations of René Lalique in the 1920s and 1930s. Phillips, New York

Figure 189. Vase in cire perdue glass, 1921, incised 321–21, height 6½ in. (17.2 cm.).

This is a late example of Lalique's naturalistic treatment of flora. In modeling the rose petals Lalique exploited the *cire perdue* process to a daring extent, achieving a degree of undercutting which would not be possible through conventional casting. *Collection of Robert and Karen Ettinger*

Figure 190. "Oran" vase in clear and frosted glass, circa 1926, wheel-cut R. LALIQUE FRANCE, height 10½ in. (26 cm.).

The stylized treatment of the peonies which decorate this vessel is typical of Lalique's floral designs of the mid-1920s. *Collection of Mr. and Mrs. Shep Porter*

Belle Epoque, and clearly inspired by the results of casting glass in the *cire perdue* technique (Figure 186). By the early 1920s, Lalique's figures, made with sophisticated methods of press molding and casting, became geometrically stylized in the Art Deco manner (Figure 187). The process of stylization and symmetrical arrangement eventually became a process of simplification of line, resulting in the uninspiring sculptures, typical of René Lalique's later designs and those of his son, Marc, from the 1950s (Figure 188).

Lalique's treatment of naturalistic forms evolved in parallel with his figural work. Although he continued to depict throughout his career the familiar droopy and exotic flora favored by the Art Nouveau designers, after 1920 he made increasing use of those flowers that lent themselves to geometric arrangement and stylization—marguerites, peonies, etc.—and developed a fascination with the geometrics of overlapping leafage (Figures 190 and 191).

Lalique's *cire perdue* work, most of which was inscribed with the year of manufacture after 1919, provides a valuable record of the evolutionary style, the progress of which is more difficult to chart in production designs, which were often manufactured over a long period of years and rarely have established dates of origin. The "rose" vase in Figure 189, made in 1921, is one of the last examples of Lalique's completely naturalistic treatment of flora. To achieve the superbly modeled collar of roses, Lalique exploited the

*cire perdue* technique, which, unlike conventional casting, allows for undercutting in a design, to a daring degree. By the mid-1920s Lalique's floral designs were stylized and geometrically arranged almost to the point of abstraction (Figure 192), a trend in decorative art which prompted adverse reaction from, among others, the French designer Paul Iribe, who asked in 1930: "For thousands the flower is as necessary as the machine; shall we sacrifice the flower on

*Figure 192. "Picardie" vase in pearlescent white glass, circa 1927, engraved R. Lalique France, height 9½ in. (24 cm.).*

Lalique's increasing use of stylization and geometric arrangement led to designs that bordered on abstraction by the mid-1920s.

*Figure 191. "Moissac" vase in amber glass, circa 1925, wheel-cut R. LALIQUE, height 5½ in. (13 cm.). Phillips, New York*

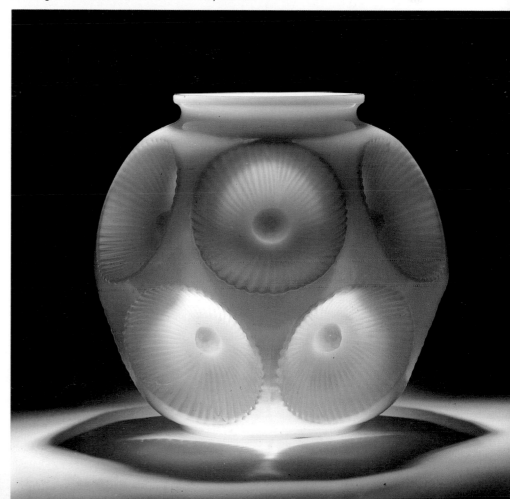

*Figure 193. "Nanking" vase in clear glass with black enamel detailing, circa 1926, engraved Lalique, height 13 in. (33 cm.).*

Lalique introduced a few vases with purely geometric decoration in the late 1920s. "Nanking" is one of the rare geometric designs of mold-blown manufacture. *Bonhams, London*

heads, their attractiveness, is fully exploited. The vase can be considered a splendid example of Lalique's mature design skills and "le style Lalique." The trend of stylization led to full geometric designs of the late 1920s and 1930s, with all traces of naturalistic forms absent from the decoration (Figure 193).

Lalique occasionally deviated from his principal sources of inspiration—flora and fauna, the aquatic world, Japonisme, neoclassicism, and the human form—to derive motifs from a current fad, partly no doubt in the interests of commercialism. During the mid-1920s the culture of the South American Indians become a subject of fascination in France. Under the promotional guidance of societies and publications, including the *Revue de l'Amérique Latine*, first published

*Figure 194. "Koudor" vase in clear glass with black enamel detailing, circa 1926, molded R. LALIQUE, height 6½ in. (18 cm.).*

The form and zigzag decoration of "Koudor" are derived from American Indian art, the geometric patterns of which were easily integrated with the French Art Moderne style.

the altar of Cubism and the machine?" Like Iribe, René Lalique never lost sight of the inherent beauty in flowers. The vase "Picardie" (Figure 192), designed in 1926, is a good example of near-abstraction in floral decoration, although the form of the poppy

in 1922, the "ignored continent" was visited, studied, excavated, and recorded. The geometric patterns of the Indians were easily integrated into the French Art Moderne style, and used by Lalique in three vases with black enamel decoration,[4] including the vase "Koudor" (Figure 194), which is the only model to have the form of Pueblo Indian pottery.

Another anomalous group of designs from the same period are those patterned with fossil formations. It is not known whether René Lalique was a student of geology or fossils, but several vase designs suggest he drew from specimens (Figure 195).

Another extraordinary design is the vase "Davos" (Figure 197), dating from the early 1930s. The graduated spheres which decorate the vessel are molded in a geometric pattern unmistakably similar to the arrangement of molecular structure as seen under microscopic conditions. It is quite possible that Lalique's design was inspired by the discoveries of the early age of nuclear physics[5] and that, in "Davos," he

*Figure 195. "Palissy" vase in charcoal-gray glass, circa 1922, molded R. LALIQUE, height 6½ in. (16.5 cm.). Phillips, New York*

*Figure 196. "Sully" standish in frosted glass with black enamel detailing, circa 1927, length 9½ in. (25 cm.).*

The primitive appeal of this design is derived from the geometric sawtooth motif, arranged in the manner of Aztec art.

Figure 197. "Davos" vase in purplish glass, circa 1932, stenciled R. LALIQUE FRANCE, height 11½ in. (29 cm.). Crystal Galleries

Figure 198. Vase in cire perdue glass, 1921, incised 272–21, height 6½ in. (17 cm.).

The slender, ovoid form of this vessel is typical of Lalique's smaller *cire perdue* vases of the early 1920s. The fish and waves are modeled in the manner of the Japanese artists Hokusai and Hiroshige. *Private collection, England*

Figure 199. Detail of Figure 198.

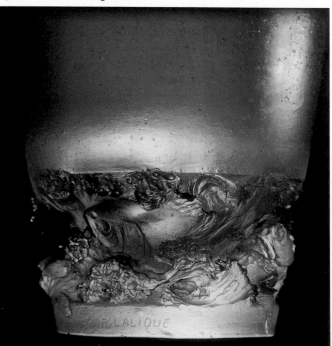

intended to express the excitement of this pioneer technology as he expressed the thrills of speed in automobile mascots.

Lalique's love of animal decoration lasted throughout his career. In his early glass and jewelry he showed a particular fondness for ugly and grotesque creatures—serpents, frogs, beetles and other insects,

Figure 200. "Poissons" vase in red glass, circa 1922, molded R. LALIQUE, height 9½ in. (24 cm.).

Lalique's decorative use of monstrous fish, including many species of carp, can be attributed to the influence of Japonisme. *Collection of A. J. Tobias*

Figure 201. "Penthièvre" vase in blue glass, circa 1927, stenciled R. LALIQUE and engraved France, height 10 in. (25.5 cm.).

By the late 1920s Lalique had abandoned the naturalistic modeling of fish in favor of a stylized, geometric treatment.

and fish, especially carp and bullheaded species. The preference for insects and fish can be attributed to the influence of Japonisme on Lalique, who continued to depict fish in the manner of Japanese artists, notably Hokusai and Hiroshige, until the mid-1920s (Figures 198, 199, and 200). By this time, however, the predominant treatment of fish decoration was a stylized, geometric arrangement (Figure 201), reaching a point of near-abstraction in the late 1920s in parallel with floral design.

By the early 1920s Lalique's preference for grotesque creatures had been superseded by his use of the more graceful and exotic animals associated with the "age of elegance"—greyhounds, birds, African game, and all manner of *les biches*, which Lalique contorted in the fashionable, mannerist style of the early Art Deco period (Figures 202 and 203). The evolutionary progression in Lalique's treatment of animals reached maturity with the design of the vase "Serpent" in 1924 (Figure 206). The coiled serpent motif was not new to French decorative art, nor to Lalique, who had first employed it on a glass vessel in 1898 (Figure 9), but in the "Serpent" vase Lalique promoted the snake from its function as a decorative element to become both the decoration and form of the vessel. The result of this unique and highly innovative design concept is one of the Art Deco period's classic creations and a powerful example of "le style Lalique."

The "Serpent" vase represents a significant break from Lalique's characteristic use of Japanese vase forms, the choice of which can be attributed to both the influence of Japonisme and to the mold-blowing method of manufacture, which, simply defined, required the blowing of a bubble of molten glass into a

*Figure 202. "Chamois" vase in amber glass, circa 1929, stenciled R. LALIQUE FRANCE, height 5 in. (12.5 cm.).*

During the 1920s the grotesque creatures of Lalique's early designs were gradually usurped by the more graceful animals and birds associated with the "age of elegance." The *biches* in this design are modeled in the elongated "mannerist" style of contemporary taste and cleverly arranged in a geometric pattern. *Collection of Mr. and Mrs. V. James Cole*

*Figure 203. "Aigrettes" vase in bronze-colored glass, circa 1927, wheel-cut R. LALIQUE FRANCE, height 9½ in. (25 cm.).*

Egrets were another favorite design motif during the late 1920s, charged with exotic appeal and natural elegance. *Collection of Glenn and Mary Lou Utt*

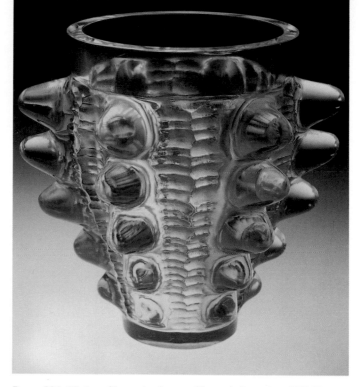

*Figure 204. "Oursin" (Sea Urchin) vase in clear and frosted glass, circa 1929, stenciled R. LALIQUE FRANCE, height 7¼ in. (27.5 cm.).*

René Lalique occasionally deviated from his favored Japanese forms to model naturalistic shapes in blown glass, always choosing objects with natural symmetry, such as this sea urchin.

*Figure 205. "Paimpol" vase in clear and frosted glass, circa 1933 (Design No. 12.240), wheel-cut R. LALIQUE, height 10 in. (26 cm.).*

This rare vessel also derives its form from a common sea urchin. *Crystal Galleries*

metal mold, and was particularly suitable for producing narrow-necked vessels of swelling form (Figures 207 and 208). The majority of Lalique's mold-blown vessels are "decorated forms," the form being the most important feature, and it is significant that Lalique never fashioned free forms, floriforms, or abstract shapes, unlike the majority of his glassmaking contemporaries, even in his unique *cire perdue* vessels made in studio conditions. This aspect of René Lalique's style is one of the fundamental differences be-

tween his designs and those of his son, Marc, and granddaughter, Marie-Claude. In his few designs of "organic" form, Lalique chose to model objects with natural symmetry, including the sea urchin from which the vase "Oursin" derives its shape (Figure 204).

After the establishment of the Wingen Glassworks in 1921, Lalique made increasing use of the press-molding method of manufacture. The technique had the advantages of producing an extremely sharp out-

*Figure 206. "Serpent" vase in purple glass, circa 1924, molded R. LALIQUE, height 10¼ in. (26 cm.).*

In this extraordinary design the coiled serpent successfully constitutes the form and decoration of the vessel. This model is normally found in frosted glass but is also recorded in opalescent, gray, amber, and this rare violet color. *Christie's, New York*

Figure 208. "Perruches" (Parakeets) vase in amber glass, circa 1923, molded R. LALIQUE, height 10 in. (25.5 cm.).

Many of Lalique's mold-blown vases are simply decorated Japanese forms, with shallow relief patterns which rarely interrupt the pleasing outline.

Figure 207. "Acanthes" vase in blue glass, circa 1924, molded R. LALIQUE, height 11 in. (28 cm.).

Lalique favored Japanese forms in vases made by the mold-blowing process, which was particularly suitable for producing narrow-necked vessels of swelling form.

Figure 209. "Tourbillons" (Whirlwinds) vase in clear glass with black enamel detailing, circa 1925, wheel-cut R. LALIQUE FRANCE, height 8 in. (20 cm.).

"Tourbillons" is René Lalique at his best, designed for mass production but comparable to the studio glass of Maurice Marinot. In the late 1920s "Tourbillons" was available in clear or colored glass (Figures 81 and 82). The black enameling was optional, available for an additional cost of 100 francs.

line in relief decoration and allowing for heavier walls and greater thicknesses of solid glass in designs. In 1925 Lalique proved he had mastered the technique when he exhibited the vase "Tourbillons" (Figure 209) at the Paris Exposition in the category of "artist-designed industrial glass." The vase shows a complete command of the technique—the sharply defined outlines, daring depth of relief, and bold, simple form, fully complementary and in period taste. "Tourbillons" is an Art Deco masterpiece, designed for mass production but comparable to the studio glass of Maurice Marinot. It is "le style Lalique" at its best, a superb technical achievement and perhaps Lalique's most mature design.

# 5. A NEW COMMERCIALISM (1930–1945)

René Lalique was seventy years old in 1930 and suffering from an arthritic complaint which had first appeared in the 1920s. Despite this handicap he continued to spearhead the company as its sole designer for the next fifteen years and maintained a reclusive lifestyle in the *hôtel* at 40 Cours la Reine. In May 1930 Lalique's indomitable behavior was described in *Fortune* magazine:

> . . . The center of modern glass craftsmanship is in France. There, René Lalique, slender, trimmoustached, with the look of a scholar, is hard at work in his Paris atelier. He is drawing designs for every sort of object: bowls, perfume bottles, doorknobs, chandeliers, candelabra, intaglio seals, dinner plates—and all to be executed by his hundreds of glass craftsmen.[1]

Lalique's work force of "glass craftsmen" consisted of about six hundred employees in 1930,[2] up from a little over four hundred in 1926,[3] and production levels were at their highest in the company's history. The impressive list of objects in *Fortune* is somewhat misleading, however. The great majority of output in 1930 consisted of old designs (some dating to the pre-1915 period). New designs for production, largely limited to vases and table glass, had actually decreased in number.

As the Lalique Company entered the new decade it also entered a newly structured marketplace for decorative glass. Contemporary interior designers saw little merit in Lalique's earlier, ornamental ware, and the large vases and *surtouts* which had complemented decor in the 1920s were unwelcome among the stark lines of modernist ensembles. Demand for de luxe

Figure 210. Portrait of René Lalique, aged about sixty-five.

Although suffering from a severe arthritic complaint, René Lalique continued to serve as the sole designer of his company's glassware until his death in 1945.

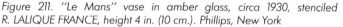

Figure 211. "Le Mans" vase in amber glass, circa 1930, stenciled R. LALIQUE FRANCE, height 4 in. (10 cm.). Phillips, New York

Figure 212. Vase patterned with stylized shorebirds in flight, amber glass, circa 1932, stenciled R. LALIQUE FRANCE, height 6½ in. (16.5 cm.). Phillips, New York

glass decreased as the worldwide Depression reduced the number of private buyers, and the Lalique Company, together with many of its contemporaries, tailored its products accordingly and sought more employment from commercial patrons.

Cost factors in production became increasingly important and items or techniques with high production overheads were discontinued or discouraged, including the manufacture of large chandeliers, mold-blown vases, and *surtouts*, the use of colored glass, and the introduction of new designs in general. *Cire perdue* work was also discontinued by 1930, possibly because of René Lalique's arthritic complaint. Large, mold-blown vase designs of the early 1920s were made on a limited scale in old molds, and the few blown vessels of new design were extremely small (Figures 211, 212,

and 213). The company experimented with new methods of blowing glass at Wingen, producing a few vessels of thin wall resembling oversized drinking glasses. The vase "Beaulieu" (Figure 214) is a good example of this genre, designed in the period taste as defined in the magazine *Good Furniture and Decoration* in 1929:

> The principal tendency in [modern glass] is to avoid all overcharging of decoration in the upper part of the glass. On the rare occasions it is ornamented we find a very light and dainty etching that forms a narrow edge or border.[4]

The 1930s was the decade of press-molded vases, which could be manufactured inexpensively and expediently, and a multitude of new designs appeared at a rate of up to a dozen per annum.[5] The vases fall

*Figure 213. "Bresse" vase in amber glass, circa 1930, stenciled R. LALIQUE FRANCE, height 4½ in. (10.5 cm.).*

This model is one of a "family" of small, mold-blown vases designed around 1930 and characterized by crisply modeled, stylized patterns with deep, frosted recesses. The usual colors are clear, lime-green, or amber and all pieces are marked with a stenciled signature (see also Figures 202, 211, and 212).

into two general categories, those made in the company tradition as decorative objects to be displayed and enjoyed for their own attractiveness (Figure 215), and a new kind of Lalique vase, designed as a vessel for holding flowers and especially suitable as a table centerpiece. The former category is characterized by a propensity for simple, conical forms, an almost exclusive use of clear or pale opalescent glass, and a general "sterility" in design (Figure 216). Decoration is typically symmetrical or repeating, with all figural or organic forms heavily stylized. Many models of similar

appearance were manufactured, including a group of a dozen small, bucket-shaped vessels, molded with projecting areas of stylized foliage. A more interesting group of vases was modeled as "rocket ships" of bullet shape, molded with projecting fins, presumably inspired by the pioneer jet-engine technology of the period.

The general trend was toward a cheap, "expendable" model which stayed in production for a limited time only. Reduction in design quality was the inevitable result of a combination of forced proliferation, the stylistic restrictions of press-molding, the absence of colored glass, and René Lalique's failing health.

*Figure 214. "Beaulieu" vase in blue glass, circa 1929, engraved R. Lalique France No. 960, height 6½ in. (17.2 cm.).*

Lalique introduced sophisticated techniques of blowing vessels at the Wingen Glassworks in the late 1920s, developed from his successes in stemware manufacture. *Collection of A. J. Tobias*

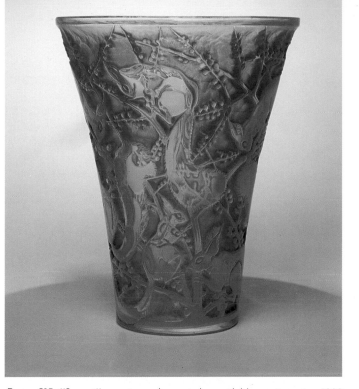

*Figure 215. "Senart" vase in opalescent glass with blue patine, circa 1932 (Design No. 1098), stenciled R. LALIQUE FRANCE, height 8¼ in. (21 cm.).*

"Senart" is one of Lalique's more attractive and complex designs of the 1930s. The decoration is unusual for a press-molded vase and more akin to the large, mold-blown designs of a decade earlier.

Among the better vase designs of the 1930s are the models "Terpsichore" (Figure 217), which is of innovative and impressive form, "Carmargue" (Figure 218), which is strong in design and fully representative of its period, and "Actina" (Figure 221), decorated with the "zipper" forms which appear on a number of Lalique vases designed in the mid-1930s. Many vases have no apparent stylistic precedent in the work of René Lalique, and it is possible that Marc Lalique may have been responsible for a few designs, including the "Actina" vase, which is typical of his own "engineered" style and can be compared to the "Ingrid" vase, designed by him in the 1960s (Figure 243).

As the purely ornamental vase receded from fashion in the 1930s, the Lalique Company began to manufacture a range of vases intended for floral displays (Figures 219 and 223). Typically, these vessels were of plain or faceted funnel shape, decorated at the base or support, or with projecting handles. The complex forms of these new vases were made possible by improvements in the press-molding technique, intro-

*Figure 216. Press-molded vase in opalescent glass, mid-1930s, stenciled R. LALIQUE FRANCE, height 6 in. (15.5 cm.).*

This model is typical of Lalique's simplistic, linear designs of the mid- to late 1930s. Most vases are in clear glass, sometimes with a pale opalescent tint as in this example. *Phillips, New York*

Figure 217. "Terpsichore" vase in opalescent glass, circa 1934 (Design No. 10.911), stenciled R. LALIQUE FRANCE, length 12½ in. (31.5 cm.).

"Terpsichore" is one of Lalique's more adventurous designs from the mid-1930s. The five-digit consecutive design numbering system was introduced around 1933 and continues to the present day. Phillips, New York

duced during the early 1930s and described in the magazine L'Européen in 1934:

> The relatively new technique of pressing glass is commonly used [in the French decorative glass industry]. It consists of pressing and molding the glass, with aid of compressed air, into hollow steel molds. The process makes possible the manufacture of inexpensive

products which resemble de luxe articles. However, this does not affect the quality of French art glass. The finest handcraftsmanship is still employed in the finishing process, including etching by acid or sand blast, frosting, polishing, and cutting. These are the features which identify fine French glass throughout the world.[6]

Despite Lalique's mastery of the press-molding technique, the company adopted a conservative approach to decorative glass manufacture, as expressed in L'Européen. The use of acid-etching increased and cut, or taillé, decoration was introduced for the first time in the company's history in about 1931. Lalique's demi-cristal was soft, with a low metallic content, and

Figure 218. "Carmargue" vase in clear glass with sepia patine, mid-1930s, stenciled R. LALIQUE, height 11¼ in. (29 cm.). Phillips, New York

*Figure 219. ''Enfants'' vase in clear and frosted glass, circa 1931, stenciled R. LALIQUE FRANCE, height 10½ in. (27 cm.).*

This goblet-shaped vessel is typical of the complex designs for flower vases made by improved press-molding techniques in the 1930s. ''Enfants'' was also offered as a table lamp, fitted with a frosted glass shade of inverted bucket shape.

unsuitable for cutting, and a new glass was used for some models. In fact, many of the *taillé* vases were not cut at all but press-molded into sharp-edged, faceted designs resembling traditional cut glass, and buffed and polished by hand to a ''crystal'' finish (Figure 223).

In 1933 a retrospective exhibition of René Lalique's glass artistry was held at the Pavilion de Marsan in the Musée des Arts Décoratifs in Paris, an extraordinary event in the history of the museum and a remarkable tribute to a living artist. A variety of flower vases with *taillé* decoration were included in the exhibition,[7] together with representative examples of jewelry and all types of glassware, displayed in dozens of vitrines and on Lalique tables, including a re-creation of a table set with glassware which had originally been displayed at the Paris Exposition of 1925.[8]

Dominating the exhibition was an enormous glass altar, fronted by an altar rail patterned with lilies and surmounted by a towering reredos molded with six

*Figure 220. Commemorative plaque from Lalique's exhibition at the Pavilion de Marsan in 1933, acid-etched clear glass, height 3½ in. (9 cm.) Collection of Mr. and Mrs. V. James Cole*

Figure 221. "Actina" vase in opalescent glass with blue patine, circa 1933 (Design No. 10.889), stenciled R. LALIQUE FRANCE, height 10¼ in. (26 cm.).

The combination of opalescent glass and pale blue patination is common in vases made in the 1930s. Some vases of "Actina" type were decorated with acid etching.

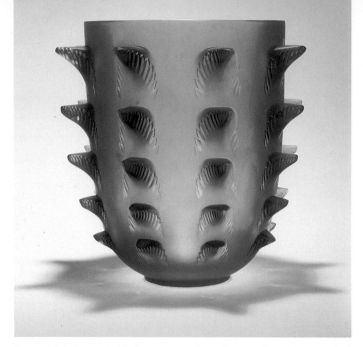

Figure 222. Press-molded vase in amber glass, early 1930s, stenciled R. LALIQUE FRANCE, height 7¼ in. (18.5 cm.).

The use of colored glass is rare in vases of 1930s design. *Weinstein Collection*

figures of angels. The assemblage, which was constructed entirely of frosted glass panels, was a larger version of the high altar designed by René Lalique for a chapel in Normandy,[9] his first ecclesiastical commission, which was installed in 1930. Owing to the expense of casting molds for structural glass panels and the uniqueness of most architectural commissions, it was a company policy to display architectural settings and interior designs at exhibitions in order to attract new patrons.

Variations of the Normandy altar were exhibited at the Salon d'Automne in 1930 and the Salon des Artistes Décorateurs in the following year prior to being shown at the Pavilion de Marsan. The exposure

earned Lalique his second, and largest, ecclesiastical commission in 1934, the renovation of St. Matthew's Church, located at Millbrook on the British Channel island of Jersey. The renovation work was sponsored by Florence Lady Trent, a local resident, in memory of her late husband, and carried out by Lalique in collaboration with the British architect A. B. Grayson.[10] Lady Trent had known René Lalique personally for a number of years prior to the commission as they owned adjacent villas in the South of France, and he had designed a pair of doors for her private home in the early 1930s.[11]

The new interior of St. Matthew's, which can still be admired today, included a high altar backed by an il-

*Figure 223. Two taillé vases of typical form, early 1930s, stenciled R. LALIQUE FRANCE, height 12½ in. (32 cm.).*

Vases of this type were intended to hold flowers and serve as table centerpieces, unlike designs of the 1920s, which were purely ornamental and nonfunctional. *Crystal Galleries*

luminated cross, an altar rail of "Jersey Lily" pattern (Figure 225), walls of glass panels enclosing an antechapel with altar and a vestry, windows, and numerous other fittings including door handles and a font (Figure 224).

Lalique's architectural commissions were not limited to ecclesiastical projects. In 1931 he designed fountains and lighting for the Exposition Coloniale in Paris and, in the same year, he was commissioned to provide glass paneling and lighting for the *Normandie*, the magnificent trans-Atlantic liner which was the largest moving object in the world when it was completed in 1935. The *Normandie*, which was tragically destroyed by fire in New York harbor in 1942, was

furnished and decorated to an unprecedented degree of extravagance and luxury by a host of *artistes décorateurs* comprising virtually every important member of the contemporary French decorative arts community, including René Lalique, the undisputed *chef*

*Figure 224. Lalique's glass font at St. Matthew's Church, Millbrook, Isle of Jersey.*

*d'oeuvre* of decorative glass. Lalique's contributions to the *Normandie* included the lighting and wall paneling in the cavernous first-class dining room, which was more than 300 feet in length, designed by the architects Paton and Pacon (Figure 226).

Figure 226. The first-class dining saloon aboard the French liner *Normandie*, circa 1935, "the largest room afloat."

The wall panels and lighting fixtures in this photograph are by Lalique. The twelve freestanding fixtures are glass fountains illuminated from within.

During the 1930s the Lalique Company found increasing commercial success in the United States, largely because of a concentrated sales campaign managed by Marc Lalique. Lalique enjoyed an enviable reputation in America, due in part to glowing reports in art journals and newspapers, including this example from a Los Angeles *Mercury* article on the opening of the Oviatt Building in 1928, which was presumably written by James Oviatt's public relations staff:

> Of particular interest to visitors to Los Angeles' newest store is the abundance of Lalique glasswork. This feature alone makes the establishment unique, as it is the first time in his long artistic career that the French genius Lalique consented to commercial creation, his creative genius being confined heretofore for use in royal palaces, notable structures of continental Europe, and objects of art treasured in museums and mansions of the world.[12]

In 1932 René Lalique completed a fourth interior design commission for an American department store[13]: the entrance lobby of John Wanamaker's in Philadelphia. The design included enormous neoclassical glass panels, framed in bronze and decorated with the sand-blasting technique (Figure 227).

In 1935, under Marc Lalique's marketing campaign, an extravagant display of Lalique glass was mounted at B. Altman's department store in New York, equal to any exhibition at the Paris salons. Altman's presenta-

*Figure 227. Panel removed from John Wanamaker's department store, Philadelphia: clear glass with sand-blasted decoration, 1932, wheel-cut R. LALIQUE 1932, 105½ in. × 58½ in. (270 cm. × 149 cm.).*

This gigantic panel is probably the largest single piece of Lalique glass in existence. Corning Museum of Glass, Corning, New York. *Gift of Benjamin D. Bernstein*

*Figure 228. "Tresor de la Mer," an opalescent glass box and cover in the form of a clamshell, circa 1939, stenciled R. LALIQUE FRANCE, and with paper label from Saks Fifth Avenue, length 6 in. (15 cm.).*

This charming model was made in an edition of fifty, exclusively for sale at Saks Fifth Avenue department store in New York during an exhibition of Lalique there in 1939. *Phillips, New York*

tion included a large selection of glassware formerly displayed at the Pavilion de Marsan in 1933, together with a variety of architectural designs including doors, mantels, wainscoting, balustrades, and fountains, a range of small objects of religious interest, and other new designs, mostly of table glass, some of which were created exclusively for Altman's.[14] Four years later the fashionable Saks Fifth Avenue store followed suit with an exclusive exhibition of Lalique glass, mostly *garnitures de toilette* (Figure 228).

Table glass manufacture proved to be an important source of revenue during the 1930s, and new patterns were continually introduced (Figures 230 and 232). With the exception of architectural panels, the use of cast glass in new designs was largely limited to small statuettes of religious subjects. An extraordinary

*Figure 229. Design for a bathtub in glass, circa 1930.*

Lalique exhibited a variety of architectural designs for private homes. This extraordinary proposal was widely exhibited from the late 1920s to the mid-1930s. *Reprinted from* New Dimensions *by Paul T. Frankl (New York, 1928).*

*Figure 230. Drinking glasses from a table service, 1930s, stenciled R. LALIQUE FRANCE.*

*The majority of Lalique's stemware patterns were of traditional design, and always executed in clear glass. Phillips, New York*

model was put into production, however, a figure of a strutting wild fowl entitled "Coq de Jungle," which was intended for use as a table centerpiece (Figure 231).

By the late 1930s Europe was recovering from the Great Depression and a spirit of optimism briefly prevailed. A new generation of "industrial designers" grew within the modernistic movement, bent on unity of form and function, art and industry, beauty and technology. The Exposition Internationale des Arts et Techniques, held in Paris in 1937, was organized to demonstrate and further these ideals, which had shaped the designs of René Lalique's glass since his first commercial venture with François Coty, thirty years earlier. At the age of seventy-seven, Lalique contributed to the exhibition by designing a commemorative medallion (Figure 233), and a glass fountain which stood in the center of the site. The fountain was of simple, hexagonal sections, composed of square blocks patterned with a design of stylized bub-

*Figure 231. "Coq de Jungle" in clear and frosted glass, circa 1936, stenciled R. LALIQUE FRANCE, height 16 in. (41 cm.).*

*Figure 232. Pair of champagne flutes, early 1930s, molded R. LALIQUE and engraved France, height 5¼ in. (13.5 cm.).*

This stylish pattern is uncharacteristically unconventional in design. The bowl and foot of each glass were blown separately and joined by a black glass knop. *Phillips, New York*

bles, a far cry from the magnificent illuminated monolith created for the Paris Exposition in 1925. The fountain represented Lalique's interpretation of industrial design, but the overall appearance was cold and sterile, lacking the subtlety of line which distinguished the sophisticated modernist designers. Sadly, Lalique applied the same approach to a number of production glass designs, which met with unfavorable reactions from contemporary critics.

The Combs-la-Ville Glassworks, faced with obsolescence and reduced demand, was closed in 1937. Three years later the Wingen factory was forced to close after the outbreak of World War II, and the plant was occupied by the Germans for the duration of the hostilities.

René Lalique died in Paris on May 9, 1945, only two days after a German delegation signed papers of unconditional surrender with the Allies in Rheims. Among the latest designs attributed to him is the bottle for Worth's Requette perfume (Figure 234), which was probably designed in the late 1930s but not released by Worth until 1946. Modeled in the form of a cog wheel, Requette is a fine example of design for an industrial age, and it is fitting to look upon this simple and inexpensive bottle as a memorial to the design genius of René Lalique.

*Figure 233. Commemorative medallion for the Exposition Internationale des Arts et Techniques, Paris, 1937; frosted glass with sepia patine, diameter 3½ in. (9 cm.). Phillips, New York*

*Figure 234. Perfume bottle for Requette fragrance by Worth, clear glass with blue enamel detailing, circa 1946, height 3½ in. (9 cm.).*

Worth introduced Requette in 1946, its first new fragrance in over seven years. The bottle, which was made in at least two sizes, was probably designed by René Lalique in the late 1930s but not put into production until after his death. *Collection of A. J. Tobias*

# 6. LALIQUE SINCE 1945: THE TRADITION CONTINUED

After the liberation of Alsace in 1945, work began on restoring and reequipping the glassworks at Wingen-sur-Moder, which had been extensively damaged during the war. René Lalique died in Paris before renovation work began, and Marc Lalique, who was already established as the plant's manager and chief administrator, inherited the roles of company figurehead and chief designer. He was shy and somewhat withdrawn, characteristics shared by his father, with an intense devotion to the family company. His technical and engineering skills had made an important contribution to production and quality control since he joined the company in 1922, and his abilities as an administrator and businessman had compensated for his father's lack of business acumen.

Marc Lalique drew upon all these qualities during the rebuilding of the Wingen Glassworks, which was completed by the late 1940s. The earliest products of the newly opened works included a combination of prewar designs, mostly figurines, paperweights, ashtrays, and table glass, together with new designs by Marc Lalique, including vases and lighting fixtures. The most significant development at the renovated factory was the introduction of a new glass mixture, containing twice the amount of lead oxide as the prewar *demi-cristal*, or about 24 percent by volume. Marc Lalique's *cristal* transformed the appearance of Lalique glass and revolutionized its methods of man-

ufacture. The new metal, which was a more expensive raw material than *demi-cristal*, was introduced to meet the demands of a postwar public who sought a clean, bright, and refreshing style in keeping with the new age of modern technology.

The production of mold-blown ware, for which the new metal was quite unsuitable, was largely discontinued, together with the use of colored glass and the application of enamels or *patine*. Opalescent glass was used into the 1950s, mostly for tableware and earlier popular designs by René Lalique (Figure 235).

*Figure 235. "Saint Marc" vase in opalescent crystal, circa 1950 (Design No. 12.221), stenciled LALIQUE FRANCE, height 6½ in. (17 cm.).*

Opalescent glass was used for the manufacture of vases, plates and bowls until the 1950s. The design of this model is attributed to René Lalique although it was not produced until after 1945.

123

*Figure 236. Portrait of Marc Lalique taken in 1977. Cristal Lalique*

uniformity which distinguished his style from that of his father.

Marc Lalique did not inherit his father's insatiable passion for designing, and the number of new designs introduced each year dwindled from several dozen during the company's heyday to less than a dozen in the 1950s. Currently, under Marie-Claude Lalique's administration, new designs are put into production at a rate of two or three a year.

Many of Marc Lalique's designs show the direct influence of his father, especially evident in his figural work (Figure 240). Statuettes and figurines are modeled in a sleek, simplistic style, lacking the striking

*Figure 237. "Coupe Antilles" in clear and frosted crystal, designed by Marc Lalique, 1950s, stenciled LALIQUE FRANCE, height 11½ in. (29.5 cm.).*

This oversized goblet is intended to hold punch. *Phillips, New York*

Despite the popularity and commercial success of René Lalique's style, Marc Lalique strove to introduce new and innovative "Laliques" and to avoid a retrospective design policy. His esthetic vision was revealed at the Art of Glass exhibition, held at the Pavilion de Marsan in 1951, which was dominated by Marc Lalique's designs, many of them making a public debut. The centerpiece of the exhibition was an enormous crystal chandelier which hung over a table set with glass dinnerware and decorations. The entire ensemble was designed by Marc Lalique, using a combination of fluid, foliate patterns and the precise realism or skillful stylizations of René Lalique, but the images are well chosen and charming.

Marc Lalique concentrated on expanding the company's retail network, seeking new and larger markets for his products, domestically and abroad. The United States became the company's most important foreign marketplace in the late 1950s, when the network of regional outlets was expanded and consolidated by Lalique's American agent and distributor, Jacques Jugeat. The prestige and mystique which Lalique glass had acquired in the United States before the war helped to generate demand for the full range of post-war products. Popular items included table glass, especially stemware (Figures 238 and 241), and all types of "giftware," including figurines, ashtrays, and small vases. Marc Lalique continued the company tradition of designing lighting fixtures, most of which were composed of frosted glass panels in the 1920s manner (Figure 244).

The design and manufacture of perfume bottles was also revived under the patronage of the Nina Ricci Company, whose fragrances, Fille d'Eve, Coeur

*Figure 238. "Ange" champagne glass in blown, etched and molded crystal, designed by Marc Lalique in 1948, height 8 in. (20.5 cm.).*

The Angel champagne glass is Marc Lalique's best-known and most popular design, inspired by medieval niche figures at Rheims Cathedral. *Cristal Lalique*

*Figure 239. Two perfume bottles and a covered box in the "Duncan" pattern, 1970s, engraved Lalique France, height of bottles 8 in. (20 cm.).*

A number of René Lalique's designs were modified by Marc Lalique and reissued after 1945. The rectangular stopper for the "Duncan" bottles is Marc Lalique's replacement for the smaller, button-shaped stopper designed by his father in the late 1920s. *Cristal Lalique*

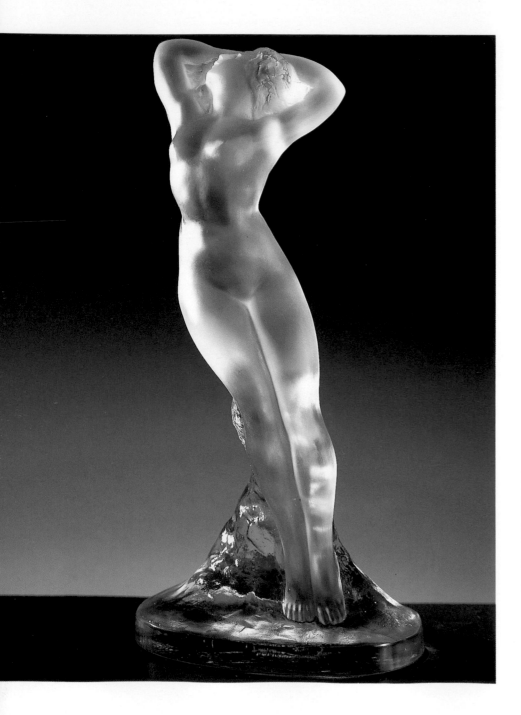

*Figure 240. "Danseuse" statuette in clear and frosted crystal, designed by Marc Lalique, 1960s, engraved Lalique France, height 9½ in. (24 cm.).*

The figural sculpture of Marc Lalique shows the strong influence of his father. This model is one of a "family" of three, including a similar figure with one arm lowered and a group of two female dancers.

Joie, and L'Air du Temps, were sold in bottles designed by Marc Lalique.

Despite the overwhelming influence of his father, Marc Lalique developed his own distinctive style which reached maturity in the early 1960s, when his best designs were created. These include a number of vases and *coupes* in brightly polished crystal with

*Figure 241. Decanter and two wineglasses in the "Roxane" pattern, designed by Marc Lalique, 1960s, engraved Lalique France.*

Table glass, especially stemware, has increased in importance as a commercial product of the Lalique Company since 1945. Many of the patterns designed by Marc Lalique are a combination of contemporary forms with decorative elements in the style of René Lalique. *Cristal Lalique*

Figure 242. "Antibes" bowl in blue crystal, 1950s, diameter 10½ in. (26.5 cm.).

The use of color is rare in Lalique glass made after 1945. This bowl is from a series of tableware with simple outline and form in the "modern" taste.

deeply gouged areas of "machined" satin finish, the finest of which is the vase "Ingrid" (Figure 243), dating from circa 1964. Marc Lalique's penchant for engineering is clearly evident in the precision molding and "engine-turned" appearance of this new genre, which represents his personal esthetics, largely unlike his father's taste, and can be compared to contemporary Scandinavian studio glass.

During the 1960s and early 1970s, Marc Lalique shared the responsibility of designing with his daughter, Marie-Claude Lalique (born 1935), who joined the company in 1956 after completing her education at the Ecole des Arts Décoratifs in Paris. As a student Marie-Claude Lalique majored in theater design, following the profession of her aunt, Suzanne Lalique

Figure 243. "Ingrid" vase in clear and frosted crystal, designed by Marc Lalique, circa 1964, engraved LALIQUE, height 10¼ in. (26 cm.).

The propellerlike design of "Ingrid" combines Marc Lalique's penchant for precision engineering with the translucent properties of crystal, in a personal style which is almost unrecognizable from that of his father. Cristal Lalique

*Figure 244. "Chêne" (Oak) chandelier or ceiling light fixture, designed by Marc Lalique, 1950s, height 12½ in. (32 cm.).*

The oak leaf was a favorite decorative element of Marc Lalique's, which he first used on lighting fixtures and a sumptuous dining table exhibited at the Pavilion de Marsan in 1951. A smaller ceiling fixture and a wall applique complete the range of lighting in the "Chêne" pattern. *Cristal Lalique*

(who also designed ceramics for the Haviland Company of Limoges), but she soon began to apply her talents to glass.

Working in the elegant and stimulating environment of her Paris atelier, located in her grandfather's *hôtel* at 40 Cours Albert 1er, or from her studio at the Wingen Glassworks, Marie-Claude Lalique creates two or three new designs for production each year in a style she has described as "within the Lalique mode."[1] As a third-generation glass designer, she is

*Figure 245. "Cygne" (Swan) figures in clear and frosted crystal, designed by Marc Lalique, 1950s, engraved Lalique France, length 13½ in. (35 cm.) and 12½ in. (31.5 cm.).*

The elegant swan was the most popular decorative bird of the 1950s, replacing the exotic species favored by René Lalique and his Art Deco contemporaries. These models are in current production, available individually or mounted on a mirrored plateau as shown. *Cristal Lalique*

Figure 246. "Bélier Amon" (Ram of Amon) in clear and frosted crystal, designed by Marie-Claude Lalique, circa 1981, engraved Lalique France, length 8 in. (20 cm.).

The design of "Bélier Amon" was inspired by Egyptian statuary, which fascinated Marie-Claude Lalique on her visit to Egypt in 1980. *Cristal Lalique*

her father's position as chief administrator, preferring the creative role of her grandfather, and by the late 1970s her repertoire of production designs included figures, decanters and other tableware, *coupes*, and more than a dozen vases in clear and colored crystal. Many of her most successful and mature designs are found in the "Singing Colors" range, introduced in the early 1970s, which consists of vases and *coupes* in free-blown crystal, decorated with colored glass motifs in relief (Figure 248). The series illustrates Marie-Claude Lalique's versatility and influences as a designer, and her abilities as a sculptor in glass. Most of her images

Figure 247. Marie-Claude Lalique with a souffleur at the Wingen Glass-works, 1982.

The modern factory employs 450 people, most of whom are engaged in production. The glassblower in this photograph is working on a "Santorin" vase, introduced in July 1981. *People*, January 11, 1982. Photo: Pierre Boulat.

especially conscious of the importance of preserving the "Lalique mode" or "le style Lalique," as it became known in the 1920s. Her approach to glass design is innovative and personal, showing a stronger influence of her father than of her grandfather, and a thorough understanding of the properties of her material. Marie-Claude Lalique's designs include a series of twelve annual plates, produced in limited editions for the American collectors' market. The first plate, en-titled "Deux Oiseaux," was introduced in September 1965 in an edition of two thousand, and the series was completed in 1976 with an "American Independence" plate featuring a heraldic eagle.

In the family tradition, Marie-Claude Lalique became the company's sole designer after the death of Marc Lalique in the winter of 1977. She did not take

are derived from nature, though she includes abstract and even neoclassical motifs in a few designs. Her work is more fluid than her father's and the influence of her grandfather is present in several models, including the vase "Santorin" (Design No. 12306), introduced in 1981, which closely resembles a René Lalique design "Vase avec Oreilles" (Design No. 927) from the early 1920s.

The continued success of the Lalique Company relies heavily on the strength of its new designs and thus on the creative talents of Marie-Claude Lalique. Her own thoughts on the company's future and the evolutionary path of "le style Lalique" were revealed in a recent interview:

> We [the company] are very aware of the styles of both my father and my grandfather. We absolutely will not do any design that "conflicts" with these styles. . . . We are now looking at the present and toward the future, but no longer at the past.[2]

*Figure 248. "Antinea" vase in clear and opalescent green crystal, designed by Marie-Claude Lalique, mid-1970s, wheel-cut LALIQUE, height 8 in. (20 cm.).*

Marie-Claude Lalique revived the use of colored and opalescent glass in her "Singing Colors" range, introduced in the early 1970s. *Cristal Lalique*

*Figure 249. A recent photograph of the Lalique Company's main Paris showroom on the Rue Royale.*

The "Cactus" table, which was designed by Marc Lalique in the early 1950s, forms the centerpiece of the company's finer showrooms and is the most expensive production model. Approximately twenty tables are sold annually in the United States. *Cristal Lalique*

# 7. ADVICE FOR THE COLLECTOR: HOW TO AVOID DEFECTS, FAKES, AND FORGERIES

On February 9, 1980, a *cire perdue* figure of a cougar (Figure 53) changed hands at a New York auction for just under $44,000, a world record for Lalique glass, which has not been broken since, despite a number of close contenders such as the "Scarab" box (Figure 29), sold in New York in December 1984 for $31,000, a record for a Lalique production design. The staggering prices commanded by rare Lalique glass, coupled with the ever-present demand for even the humblest examples, have led to the inevitable appearance of specious imitations in the collectors' marketplace. The imitation of Lalique glass is not a modern phenomenon; during the 1920s, Lalique's rise to fame brought forth a flood of inferior imitations in its wake, most of them manufactured in France or Bohemia. The Lalique-style glass of the 1920s and 1930s, the majority of which is made in frosted or opalescent glass, falls into two categories: pieces made in contemporary taste and loosely in the manner of Lalique, and pieces made to resemble Lalique production designs and offered as "poor man's Lalique" in direct competition with the genuine article, often through misleading or confusing advertising.

The former category comprises the great majority of Lalique-style glass. Most of these items were inno-

cently and honestly manufactured to satisfy contemporary demand, and only benefited indirectly from Lalique's successes, which had helped to generate

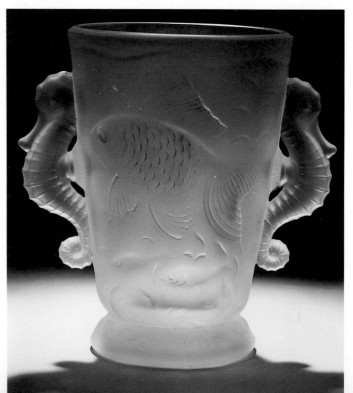

Figure 250. *Lalique-style vase in frosted glass, probably French, 1930s, bears engraved signature R. Lalique, height 8 in. (20 cm.).*

Inexpensive, press-molded vases of this type were manufactured in large numbers from the 1930s to the 1950s and were commonly used by florists. The spurious signature was probably added during the 1970s.

132

demand in the first place. This ware consists of everything from figurines, vases, and table glass to lighting fixtures and even architectural panels. Lalique-style glass of French origin varies in quality from inexpensive flea market ware to the well-designed products of specialist glassmakers, including André Hunebelle, Verlys, and Maurice-Ernest Sabino, whose opalescent glass and lighting fixtures are often comparable in quality to Lalique's later work. The majority of French glass by established manufacturers was signed, and is rarely passed off as Lalique nowadays since it is widely collected for its own merit. Lalique's French glassmaking contemporaries worked in a form of *demi-cristal* which can be difficult to distinguish from his own glass, especially when used in molded or etched panels of the type used in lighting fixtures, which Lalique rarely signed.

Lalique-style glass from Czechoslovakia is much easier to identify since the Bohemians used a metal of higher lead content for their clear and frosted ware, making it brighter, clearer, and sharper in outline than Lalique's glass. There were about 300 glassworks operating in Bohemia during the 1920s, a number of which specialized in decorative glass of Lalique type, mostly made for export to Europe and the United States. The vase illustrated in Figure 251 is a typical example, and was probably made in the interwar period, although glass of this type is still in production today. Bohemian designers were particularly fond of the bacchanalian female nudes favored by Lalique in his early career, but their figures are poorly modeled and designs rarely take advantage of the translucent properties of glass. Czechoslovakian craftsmen have traditionally excelled in the cutting of glass and many Lalique-style vases include cut and polished areas which are rarely found on the genuine article.

*Figure 251. Lalique-style vase of Bohemian (Czechoslovakian) origin, 1930s, bears engraved signature R. Lalique, height 7 in. (17.5 cm.).*

This model, also common in "malachite" glass, is frequently mistaken for the real thing. Note the poor quality of molded detail, the lack of polished relief, and the clumsy, "facet-cut" base, all of which are atypical of Lalique's work.

Differences in glass type, inferior quality, and stylistic anomalies which exist in all Lalique-style ware can be identified by any seasoned collector or cautious beginner. A greater threat is posed by the relatively small number of objects from the 1920s and 1930s which were designed to resemble or imitate Lalique production models, often so closely as to be considered forgeries. With the exception of a few vase designs in blown glass, the majority of contemporary copies are of figurines and other small, cast objects, which could be manufactured cheaply and in large

Figure 252. Figure of a bird in frosted glass, French, 1930s, molded R. LALIQUE, length 5 in. (12.5 cm.).

Lalique's bird figures were introduced in the late 1920s and have remained popular ever since. This model was manufactured by a rival company and is easily distinguishable from the genuine article by its inferior quality.

quantities. Lalique's bird models were extensively imitated (Figure 252), as were the popular and prestigious car mascots (Figure 253), copies of which were made in France, Britain, and the United States.

Glass made in the Lalique style, including direct copies of production models, is most convincing when it is signed in the manner of the genuine article. Unlike the imitation of Lalique's glass, the addition of his signature in order to "attribute" pieces is a relatively recent phenomenon, coincidental with the increase in value of Lalique glass over the last fifteen years or so. Forged Lalique signatures on glass fall into four general types, which I have called engraved editions (or dentist's-drill type), molded additions, stencil-etched additions, and modified signatures.

## Engraved Additions

The most common method of signing glassware is by engraving the finished article with a diamond-point drill. The number and styles of "Lalique" signatures applied to non-Lalique glass by this method are as many and varied as the hands that guided the drills, but signatures of this type are normally easy to recognize. An unskilled hand will always produce a wobbly signature, usually sticking to just the word *Lalique* or R. *Lalique* in order to avoid an unsightly mess. Some genuine signatures were applied in this manner and many are somewhat wobbly (Figures 52, 66, and 87), but all conform to a distinct style of handwriting. It is unfortunate that these authentic marks are often mistaken for modern forgeries. Another common form of this type is the signature applied by a skilled engraver, which is normally in impressive script and convincing in appearance. The "professional" signature is usually found on elaborate, unusual, or otherwise "rare" examples of Lalique-style ware, and may be quite wordy and informative. The author has seen several unique attributions expressed in this manner, including the remarkable *René Lalique Paris France* No. 1 1900. (The blame for this particular example can be placed squarely in the United States, where "France" always qualifies "Paris" in a sentence.) Engraved additions are easily applied and constitute the largest category of forged signatures.

*Figure 253. Automobile mascot with original mount in frosted glass, made in England by the Red Ashay Company, circa 1930.*

This model bears a striking resemblance to the popular Lalique figure "Chrysis" (Figure 254), and was clearly intended to deceive the gullible British motorist.

*Figure 254. "Chrysis" automobile mascot in clear and frosted glass, circa 1928, stenciled R. LALIQUE FRANCE, height 5¼ in. (13.5 cm.).*

Lalique's original version is infinitely more elegant than its brazen imitator.

*Molded Additions*

Of all the methods of forging signatures, this is the most convincing. Molded signatures, considered by many to be an undisputable sign of authenticity, appear on a variety of non-Lalique glass and are a source of puzzlement to all, including the connoisseur. The number of spurious pieces manufactured with forged signatures in the mold is quite small, and all of those the author has encountered bear a large, boldface R. LALIQUE which does not conform to any recorded authentic mark. More common, and more convincing, is the "applied molded" mark, added to the finished glass, presumably with the aid of a heated metal dye. Signatures of this type normally appear on small objects, including "fancy" Art Deco perfume bottles, figurines, and bird models, spelling out R. LALIQUE in capitals. The lettering is normally poorly defined, and the glass immediately surrounding the lettering has a "molten" appearance. The placement of this type of signature is often uncharacteristic of Lalique: vertically on the wall of a perfume bottle, for example.

## Stencil-Etched Additions

This form of signature is a very recent and regrettable introduction to the world of Lalique collecting. It is a relatively easy procedure for the forger to add a mark using a metal stencil and a little hydrofluoric acid, with the added advantage of producing a uniform signature which gains credibility through recurrence. Most signatures of this type are easily recognized by their bold, crude, and often bizarre lettering, and are normally found placed in prominent positions on

*Figure 255. Stencil-etched signature of recent origin.*

The letters are crudely outlined and stand out in relief. Marks of this type are placed prominently on the unfortunate objects they misrepresent. It is not uncommon to find this signature added to a genuine example of Lalique glass which had been previously unsigned.

larger articles of glass (Figures 255 and 256). This technique has been used to misrepresent Lalique-style glass as unique exhibition pieces by Lalique, and marks—including dates, locations, and other misleading information—are recorded. As a further point of confusion, signatures of this type are sometimes found on genuine Lalique glass, which may have been previously unsigned or had the original marks removed, and are also found on Lalique crystal made since 1945. It should be noted that stencil-etched signatures of this type, with the lettering raised, have never been used by the Lalique Company. The small stenciled R. LALIQUE FRANCE signature, used by Lalique during the 1930s, has been reproduced in recent years with alarming success. This form of forged stenciled mark has been found on small objects of non-Lalique origin, including bird models in colored glass. A close examination of this signature type reveals a slight fuzziness to the outline of an otherwise perfect forgery, which would convince the majority of buyers and many collectors.

The mixture of boldness and appalling graphics in this example can only be considered as impudence on the forger's part. This signature was found on a perfectly respectable Art Deco vase made by the Belgian firm of Val Saint Lambert.

*Figure 257. Engraved signature of a type found on a wide range of Lalique glassware made between 1945 and about 1960.*

*Figure 258. Two examples of the "Daim" (Deer) paperweight in clear and frosted glass, circa 1930 (left) and 1975, molded R. LALIQUE FRANCE and engraved Lalique France respectively, height 3¼ in. (8 cm.).*

A number of prewar designs were made after 1945, using the original molds with signatures removed. Lalique crystal (*right*) has a bright, clear appearance with sharp edges, poor definition in molding, and a smooth, satiny finish in frosted areas. In contrast, the *demi-cristal* figure is "warmer," with more fluidity, softer edges, and finer detail in molding. *Crystal Galleries*

## Modified Signatures

After René Lalique's death in 1945, the initial "R" was omitted from signatures and marks, which otherwise remained much the same as before (Figure 257). It is a relatively common practice to promote glass made after 1945 to prewar status by placing an "R" before the engraved or stenciled Lalique signature, especially on objects of René Lalique design which remained in production after 1945. The new initials are normally easy to spot and, in any event, Lalique glass

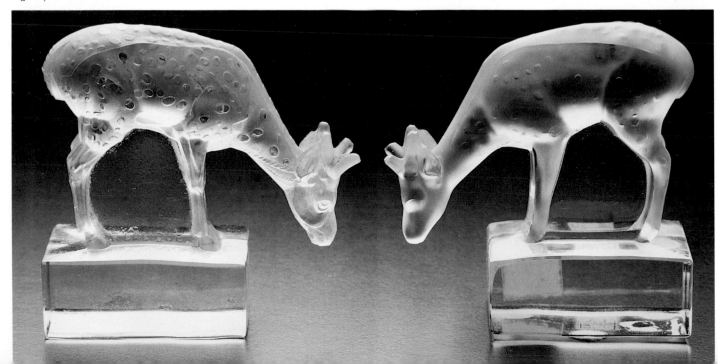

made since 1945 is of a different nature from—and easily distinguishable from—prewar *demi-cristal* (Figure 258).

It should be noted that a few Lalique models made after 1945 are signed R. LALIQUE. These include a small number of automobile mascots made as paperweights in the 1950s in old molds with the signature left in (all examples were also engraved *Lalique France*). In recent years the automobile mascot "St. Christophe" has been reissued, complete with its intaglio molded R. LALIQUE signature, and can only be distinguished from the original by glass type.

It is unfortunate that the most likely victims of the forger's craft are novice collectors, many of whom will be dissuaded from continuing the pursuit of Lalique after the inevitable discovery that they have been stung. The seasoned veteran enjoys picking his way through the barrage of "wrong" pieces placed on the

*Figure 259. "Amiens" vase in frosted glass, circa 1930, wheel-cut R. LALIQUE FRANCE, height 7½ in. (18 cm.).*

In this restored model of "Amiens" the two lower spirals have been removed and the stumps rounded off into a modified version of the design.

market by ignorant or unscrupulous dealers, flea market stall holders, auctioneers, collectors, and even museums. Sidestepping forgeries is part of the colorful collecting game, and the pleasures inherent in discovering fakes should not be underestimated. The collector who relies on his eye needs little advice, but the novice should proceed into the *caveat emptor* marketplace with utmost caution, and not be afraid to seek reliable advice before making a purchase. It is remarkable how many objects change hands on the strength of a signature, which can be added to any piece of glass in a matter of minutes at virtually no cost. When collecting Lalique, or any items which bear the mark or signature of the maker, it is prudent to adhere faithfully to one simple rule: Never allow a mark to authenticate a piece; rather, let the qualities of the piece—its workmanship, design, decoration, and composition—authenticate the mark!

Despite the large number of outright fakes and forgeries available, the most common source of confusion, frustration, and disappointment for the collector is the genuine article of Lalique glass which has been "modified" at some point in its history. Whenever glassware is handled it is at risk of being damaged. An inexpensive wineglass that suffers a chip is likely to be discarded, but a prized Lalique vase is more likely to be sent for restoration. A skilled restorer can remove chips by grinding and smoothing areas, or even remove an entire area of design (Figure 259). Bottles can be fitted with new stoppers to replace lost or damaged originals, cracks and holes can be hidden, and badly damaged pieces can be salvaged and transformed into something quite different—a bowl into a wall sconce, a vase into a table lamp, a perfume bottle into jewelry. The seasoned collector relies on his eye, experience, caution, and a

Figure 260. *"Tête de Coq" automobile mascot or paperweight in clear and frosted glass, circa 1929, molded LALIQUE FRANCE, height 6½ in. (16.5 cm.).*

This apparently perfect example of "Tête de Coq" has been restored in two places: The middle point of the comb has been "shaved" slightly and, more drastically, the lug that once protruded from the base to fit a metal mount has been almost entirely removed (the remaining portion, at the front, gives the figure an awkward upward tilt). Note the signature, without the initial "R," which is peculiar to this model and still used today. The correct height for "Tête de Coq" is 7¼ in. (18 cm.).

library of reference material to spot "wrong" pieces, which present enormous problems to the uninitiated.

There are no hard and fast rules for spotting repairs, but a good library and a degree of common sense will help anyone avoid them. The reprinted version of the Lalique Company catalogue of 1932[1] is a valuable tool, including photographs and dimensions of more than 1,500 designs. When examining an object for repairs it is wise to pay particular attention to protruding or irregular elements in a design, which are more susceptible to damage. Vases are less prone to chipping than objects for use, such as ashtrays, paperweights, perfume bottles, and automobile mascots. The most common repair on vases occurs at the

rim, which may have been ground on the inner or outer edge to remove small chips, or reduced in height to remove larger areas of damage. Rim grinding should not be confused with the original chamfer or bevel which was added to Lalique glass to prevent sharp edges.

Automobile mascots are more widely collected than any other category of Lalique glass. The demand from collectors, automobile enthusiasts, and museums is largely for perfect examples and far exceeds supply. Despite the remarkable durability claimed by retailers during the 1920s and 1930s, mascots have always been susceptible to minor damage, especially those with protruding or pointed elements in design. Metal mounts may hide damaged areas on bases and it is wise to remove mascots for examination. It is necessary to tread carefully in the automobile mascot marketplace, where only perfect examples command a premium price (Figures 260 and 261).

Figure 261. *"Victoire" automobile mascot in clear and frosted glass, circa 1925, molded R. LALIQUE FRANCE.*

This example of "Victoire" has been skillfully ground to remove chips from the edge of the figure's flowing hair. The length between nose and tip has been reduced by about one-half inch and the rear edge has been remodeled into a curve. A perfect example of this model is illustrated in Figure 146.

# NOTES

CHAPTER 1: THE JEWELER WHO DISCOVERED GLASS (1860–1905)

1. Henri Vever, *La Bijouterie Française au XIX me Siècle*, Vol. III (Paris: H. Floury, 1908).
2. *Ibid.*, pp. 703, 704.
3. *Ibid.*, p. 704.
4. For a more complete explanation of the *cire perdue* technique, see page 19.
5. *René Lalique: Sculptor in Glass* (New York: B. Altman and Company, 1935).
6. Vever, *op. cit.*, pp. 713, 714.
7. See Marc and Marie-Claude Lalique, *Lalique* (Paris: Société Lalique, 1977), p. 206, for an illustration of the portrait plaque of Mme. Lalique.
8. Jules Henrivaux, *La Verrerie au XX me Siècle* (Paris, 1911), pp. 572, 576.
9. André Beaunier, "Les Bijoux de Lalique au Salon," *Art et Décoration* (August 1902), p. 38.
10. *Ibid.*
11. "Les Salons de 1897: Emile Gallé," *Gazette des Beaux Arts*, Vol. XVIII (1897), p. 248.
12. Hilton Kramer, *The Sculpture of Gaston Lachaise* (New York: Eakins Press, 1967).
13. Guillaume Janneau, *Modern Glass* (London: The Studio Ltd., 1931), Chapter II.
14. Gustave Kahn, "Lalique Verrier," *Art et Décoration* (September 1912), p. 49.
15. "La Maison de René Lalique," *Art et Décoration* (November 1902), p. 162.
16. *Ibid.*, p. 161.

CHAPTER 2: THE DAWN OF AN EMPIRE (1905–1915)

1. See *L'Art Décoratif*, No. 80 (May 1905), p. 220, for an illustration of a blown-glass wine flute by Lalique.
2. See *Art et Décoration* (July 1907), p. 20, for an illustration of mold-blown goblets by Lalique.
3. Jules Henrivaux, *La Verrerie au XX me Siècle* (Paris, 1911).
4. "La Parfumerie aux Arts Décoratifs," *La Renaissance de l'Art Française et des Industries de Luxe* (July 1925).
5. "A New and Great Craftsman in France," *The Craftsman* (October 1912), p. 81.
6. Gustave Kahn, "Lalique Verrier," *Art et Décoration* (September 1912), p. 149.
7. Henri Clouzot, "Daum, Verrerie d'Art," in *Mobilier et Décoration* (December 1930).
8. Nilsen J. Lauvrik, *René Lalique—Master Craftsman* (New York: Haviland and Company, 1912).
9. Henrivaux, *op. cit.*

10. *Ibid.*, p. 571.
11. Kahn, *op. cit.*, pp. 149–58.
12. Lauvrik, *op. cit.*
13. The early 1920s date is supported by the existence of a similar vessel that was exhibited at the Pavilion de Marsan in 1922.
14. Lauvrik, *op. cit.*
15. Both examples are in American private collections.
16. See *Catalogue des Verreries de René Lalique* (Paris: Lalique et Cie, 1932), Design No. 878, pl. 8.
17. Model of "4 Masques" was given to the Musée des Arts Décoratifs, by René Lalique, in 1913, Acc. #19306.
18. See Christopher Vane Percy, *The Glass of Lalique* (New York: Charles Scribner's Sons, 1983), p. 110, fig. 127, for an illustration of the gates.
19. Collection of Laurens and Lorraine Tartasky, Crystal Galleries.

CHAPTER 3: THE IRREPRESSIBLE CREATOR (1915–1930)

1. "Lalique Glass," *International Studio* (June 1919), p. 126.
2. The date 1929 appears on a *cire perdue* vase with geometric fish design illustrated in Katharine M. McClinton, *Lalique for Collectors* (New York: Charles Scribner's Sons, 1975), p. 44. The incised number is described as F195–29, and may have been misread for 895–29, which would fit into the chronological sequence.
3. A *cire perdue* vase in the collection of the Corning Museum of Glass, Corning, New York, is inscribed No. 593 5–26 (presumably for May 1926), and is the highest number in the sequence recorded by the author.
4. Jules Henrivaux, *La Verrerie au XX me Siècle* (Paris, 1911), p. 572.
5. The curator of the Musée de Lyons, Leon Rosenthal, purchased a number of pieces of Lalique glass from the Paris Exposition of 1925.
6. Maximilian Gauthier, "Le Maître Verrier René Lalique à l'Exposition," *La Renaissance de l'Art Française et des Industries de luxe* (September 1925).
7. Miguel Zamacoïs, *Chez René Lalique* (Paris: Theo Brugière, 1928).
8. *Catalogue of Lalique Glass*, circa 1920 to 1940, Fonds Chambon Collection, Corning Museum of Glass Library, Corning, New York.
9. *Ibid.*
10. Between $6,000 and $8,000 each, according to Mrs. Gordon Stables, "Lalique," *Artwork* (May 1927), p. 33.
11. "René Lalique," *Mobilier et Décoration* (September 1925), pp. 31, 32.
12. *Catalogue of Lalique Glass*, *op cit.*
13. Zamacoïs, *op cit.*
14. *Catalogue of Lalique Glass*, *op cit.*, Design No. 1101.
15. Stables, *op. cit.*
16. *Catalogue of Lalique Glass*, *op. cit.*
17. Stables, *op. cit.*

18. Gauthier, *op. cit.*

19. *Ibid.*

20. *Ibid.*

21. L'*Exposition des Arts Décoratifs et Industriel, Rapport Génèral* (Parfumerie, Section Française) (Paris, September 1925).

22. Zamacoïs, *op cit.*

23. Stables, *op. cit.*

24. Zamacoïs, *op. cit.*

25. *Art et Industrie* (January 10, 1928).

26. Henri Verne and René Charance, L'*Art Décoratif Moderne en France* (Paris: Chez Hachette, 1925).

27. *Catalogue of Lalique Glass, op. cit.*

28. Stables, *op. cit.*

29. See Wolf Uecker, *Lampen und Leuchter* (Frankfurt, 1978), p. 117, pl. 0169, for an illustration of a table lamp by René Lalique and Edgar Brandt.

30. See Gabriel Mourey, "Lalique's Glassware," *Commercial Art* (July 1926), p. 34, for an illustration of a Lalique cornice fixture.

31. *Ibid.*, pp. 35, 36.

32. Paule Bayle, "Chez Lalique," L'*Art Décoratif*, No. 80 (May 1905), p. 220.

33. Howell S. Cresswell, "Modern Glass," *Good Furniture and Decoration* (September 1929), pp. 160, 161.

34. *La Renaissance de l'Art Française et des Industries de Luxe* (September 1925).

35. *Catalogue of Lalique Glass, op. cit.*

36. Edmond Haraucourt, *La Musée de la Double Soif.* Ed. Cusenier, Draeger, 1925.

CHAPTER 4: "Le Style Lalique": The Evolution of a Style

1. Miguel Zamacoïs, *Chez René Lalique* (Paris: Théo Brugière, 1928).

2. Maximilian Gauthier, "René Lalique," *La Renaissance de l'Art Française et des Industries de Luxe* (September 1925).

3. "The Exhibition of Monsieur Lalique," *The Studio* (July 1905), p. 18.

4. The other two models are "Nimroud" (Design No. 970) and "Lagamar" (Design No. 967).

5. The early 1930s was a period of rapid development in the understanding of nuclear structure, stimulated by the identification of new subatomic particles, including the positron and the neutron, both discovered in 1932, which received widespread publicity.

CHAPTER 5: A NEW COMMERCIALISM (1930–1945)

1. "Sand into Glass," *Fortune* (May 1930).

2. *Ibid*

3. Gabriel Mourey, "Lalique's Glassware," *Commercial Art* (July 1926), p. 34.

4. Howell S. Cresswell, "Modern Glass," *Good Furniture and Decoration* (September 1929), p. 159.

5. *Catalogue of Lalique Glass,* circa 1920–1940, Fonds Chambon Collection, Corning Museum of Glass Library, Corning, New York.

6. Paul Courville, "L'Industrie du Verre en France," L'*Européen* (June 1, 1934).

7. "L'Exposition de l'Oeuvre de René Lalique au Pavilion de Marsan," *Mobilier et Décoration* (March 1933), pp. 95–103.

8. Guy de Montgailhard, "L'Exposition de René Lalique," L'*Express du Midi* (March [?] 1933).

9. La Chapelle de la Vierge Fidèle, in Caen, Normandy.

10. Jane Ashelford, "Lalique's Glass Church," *Journal of Decorative Arts Society,* No. 4 (1980), p. 28.

11. *Ibid.*

12. "Alexander and Oviatt's New Store: Finest in America," *Los Angeles Mercury,* 1928 (undated).

13. Lalique's previous U.S. commissions included the Coty Building (1913), the Jay Thorpe Building, and the Oviatt Building (both 1928).

14. *René Lalique: Sculptor in Glass* (New York: B. Altman and Company, 1935).

CHAPTER 6: LALIQUE SINCE 1945: THE TRADITION CONTINUED

1. "An Interview with Marie-Claude Lalique," *Collector Editions* (Summer 1983), p. 25.

2. *Ibid.*

CHAPTER 7: ADVICE FOR THE COLLECTOR: HOW TO AVOID DEFECTS, FAKES, AND FORGERIES

1. *Catalogue des Verreries de René Lalique* (Paris: Lalique et Cie, 1932, reprinted New York: Dover Press, 1983).

# GLOSSARY OF TERMS

*applique*   French word for a sconce or other fitting attached to a wall or to a piece of furniture, made in a variety of designs by the Lalique Company since the early 1920s.

*artiste décorateur*   French term for an artist or craftsman specializing in creating decorative art for use in interior design. See also *ensemblier*.

*les arts mineurs*   French term meaning "the minor arts," used to distinguish all forms of art not considered "fine art" (paintings and sculpture), also "decorative arts."

*attache*   French word meaning an attachment; René Lalique's term for the molded glass tablets added to hanging chains or cords of ceiling light fixtures as optional extras.

*les biches*   French word meaning deer, used collectively to describe the gazelles, antelope, and deer favored for their elegance by Lalique and other designers during the 1920s.

*bonbonnière*   A small box for sweetmeats, made in a variety of designs by the Lalique Company since the early 1920s.

*bouchon à l'émeri*   French term for the process of "stoppering" glass vessels using carborundum powder.

*bouchons de radiateur*   French term literally translating as "radiator stoppers"; René Lalique's term for glass automobile mascots, which were often mounted on radiator caps.

*ceuilleur*   A glassworker, responsible for supervising the melting and pouring of glass; the assistant to a *souffleur*.

*chef d'oeuvre*   French term for the foremost authority or exponent in any field. René Lalique was considered the *chef d'oeuvre* of decorative glass design during the 1920s. See also *maître de l'oeuvre*.

*chef de place*   The foreman, or floor supervisor, of a glassworks or small manufactory.

*cire perdue*   A casting technique, literally translating as "lost wax," traditionally used in bronze work and applied to glass manufacture by René Lalique. The process requires modeling a master mold in wax which is encased in a ceramic mixture and baked, causing the casing to harden and the wax to melt and run off, leaving a hollow mold.

*confidence d'artiste*   French term meaning "an artist's secret," used to describe any object made by a unique or highly skilled process, including René Lalique's *cire perdue* ware.

*coupe*   French word for a large cup or bowl, including salad or fruit bowls.

*cristal*   A type of glass containing at least 24 percent lead oxide by volume, made by the Lalique Company since 1945. See also *demi-cristal*.

*dallage*   French word meaning "paving slab," first made in molded glass during the late nineteenth century. See also *pierre de verre*.

*demi-cristal*   A type of glass containing about 12 percent lead oxide by volume, made by the Lalique Company exclusively before 1945.

*ébéniste*  A French cabinetmaker specializing in the manufacture of fine quality, formal furniture using exotic woods and veneers.

*ensemblier*  French word for an interior designer or a company specializing in interior design.

*fauteuil*  An open armchair, of formal type.

*Fin-de-Siècle*  French term for the years immediately preceding 1900, used to describe certain styles in the decorative arts of that period.

*garniture de table*  A table decoration or ornament, including ornamental tableware.

*garniture de toilette*  Any decorative or ornamental object intended for dressing table or boudoir use.

*le hôme*  French word meaning "the home," or any domestic environment.

*hôtel*  French word for a hotel or hostelry, used by René Lalique's contemporaries to describe the premises at 40 Cours la Reine, probably because of the large number of visitors received there and Lalique's own use of the living quarters.

*Japonisme*  Name given to the Western interpretation of Japanese art and culture, most evident in decorative arts of the third quarter of the nineteenth century.

*jardinière*  A planter or tub-shaped vessel

*joaillier*  French word meaning a jeweler or any worker in gemstones.

*lustre*  French word for chandelier, used by the Lalique Company to describe any larger or branched ceiling light fixture.

*maître de l'oeuvre*  A *chef d'oeuvre*.

*maître verrier*  French term meaning "master glassmaker"; a label of distinction within the profession.

*maquette*  A prototype or original work of art, the wax model in *cire perdue* work for example.

*Monnaie du Pape*  French word meaning "Honesty plant," a favorite decorative element in René Lalique's designs.

*motif d'accrochage*  French term translating as "hanging motif," used by the Lalique Company to describe the decorative glass tubes which concealed chains and cords of ceiling light fixtures made during the 1920s and 1930s.

*parfumeur*  A manufacturer or purveyor of fragrances.

*pâte de verre*  French term meaning "glass paste"; a form of glass, usually of opaque, mottled coloration, made by grinding vitreous glass into a fine powder and casting it in semimolten paste form.

*patine*  French word meaning "patina," used by René Lalique to describe the colored enamel stains often added to molded glass to enhance or highlight decoration in relief.

*pendulette*  French word for a small clock, often used on desks or dressing tables in the 1920s.

*pierre de verre*  French term, literally translating as "glass stone," used to describe the heavily cast glass slabs used in architecture from the late nineteenth century. See also *dallage*.

*plafonnier*  A light fixture of bowl shape which can be hung from a ceiling or attached flush to it.

*sable*  French word for sand, the basic raw material of glass, as in the *sables de Fontainebleau* (Fontainebleau Sands) which supplied René Lalique's factory at Combs-la-Ville.

*souffleur*  French word meaning a blower or glassblower.

*surtout* An ornamental object or centerpiece designed to be placed on a dining table or sideboard, a shortened form of *surtout de table*.

*taillé* French word meaning "cut" as in "cut glass."

*tsuba* The hilt section in Japanese sword furniture terminology, having a characteristic form which René Lalique frequently copied in glass jewelry design.

*tulipe* French word used to describe a small lamp shade or chandelier globe.

*la vie au dehors* French term meaning "the outdoor life," which assumed a new importance among the liberated, sun-seeking society of post–World War I Europe.

# SELECTED BIBLIOGRAPHY

## Books (on Lalique)

Arwas, Victor. *Lalique*. New York: Rizzoli International, 1980.

Barten, Sigrid. *René Lalique: Schmuck und Objets d'Art 1890–1910*. Munich, 1977.

Bley, Alice. *A Guide to Fraudulent Lalique*. Ohio: Antique Appraisers Association, 1981.

Geoffroy, Gustave. *René Lalique*. Paris: E. Mary, 1922.

Lalique, Marc and Marie-Claude. *Lalique par Lalique*. Paris: Société Lalique, 1977.

Lauvrik, Nilsen J. *René Lalique; Master Craftsman*. New York: Haviland and Co., 1912.

McClinton, Katharine Morrison. *An Introduction to Lalique Glass*. Iowa: Wallace Homestead, 1978.

———. *Lalique for Collectors*. New York: Scribner's, 1975.

Percy, Christopher Vane. *The Glass of Lalique*. New York: Charles Scribner's Sons, 1977.

Zamacoïs, Miguel. *Chez René Lalique*. Paris: Theo Brugiére, 1928.


## Catalogues, Exhibitions, etc. (of Lalique)

*Works of René Lalique* by Gustave Kahn. Agnew's Gallery, Old Bond Street, London, 1905.

*Lalique Lights and Decorations*. Breves Galleries, London, circa 1928.

*Lalique Car Mascots*. Breves Galleries, London, circa 1928.

*Catalogue des Verreries de René Lalique*. Paris: Lalique et Cie, 1932; reprinted by Dover Press, New York, 1982.

*René Lalique: Sculptor in Glass*. New York: B. Altman and Company, 1935.

*Lalique at C.V.P.* C.V.P. (Percy) Gallery, London, 1974.

*René Lalique Glass: The Charles and Mary Magriel Collection*. Fitchburg Art Museum, Massachusetts, 1975.

*René Lalique*. Museum Bellerive, Zurich, Summer 1978.

*The Roger J. Mouré Collection of Lalique*. Phillips Auctioneers, New York, March 21, 1979.

*Lalique*. Phillips Auctioneers, New York, October 6, 1979.

*Important Lalique Glass*. Phillips Auctioneers, New York, February 9, 1980.

*Important Lalique Glass and Lalique Jewelry*. Phillips Auctioneers, New York, June 11, 1980.

*Important Lalique Glass*. Christie's Auctioneers, New York, October 1, 1980.

*Important Lalique Glass*. Christie's Auctioneers, New York, December 6, 1980.

*Sale of Lalique Glass*. Bonhams Auctioneers, London, September 27, 1984.

*René Lalique*. Parco Gallery, Tokyo, December 1982.

*Lalique Encore*. Dyansen Gallery, New York, March 1984.


## Works of General Reference

Arwas, Victor. *Glass: Art Nouveau to Art Deco*. New York: Rizzoli International, 1977.

Azaredo-Perdigao, José de. *Calouste Gulbenkian, Collector*. Lisbon: Calouste Gulbenkian Foundation, 1982.

Battersby, Martin. *The Decorative Thirties*. London: Studio Vista, 1969.

———. *The Decorative Twenties*. London: Studio Vista, 1971.

Calmettes, Pierre. *Excursions à travers les Metiers: Verreries et Cristaleries*. Paris: Felix Juven, circa 1908.

146

Calouste Gulbenkian Foundation. *Calouste Gulbenkian Museum Catalogue.* Lisbon, 1982.

Coty International. *The History of Coty.* Pamphlet. New York, 1984.

Garner, Philippe (ed.). *The Encyclopedia of Decorative Arts, 1890–1940.* New York: Van Nostrand and Reinhold, 1979.

Grover, Ray and Lee. *European Art Glass.* Vermont: Charles Tuttle, 1970.

Henrivaux, Jules. *La Verrerie au XX^me Siècle.* Paris, 1911.

Hillier, Bevis. *The World of Art Deco.* New York: E. P. Dutton, 1971.

Janneau, Guillaume. *Le Luminaire.* Paris, 1925–1928.

———. *Modern Glass.* London: The Studio Ltd., 1931.

Leseuitre, Alain. *The Spirit and Splendor of Art Deco.* Secaucus, N.J.: Castle Books, 1978.

*L'Exposition des Arts Décoratifs et Industriel. Rapport Général* (Parfumerie, Section Française). Paris, September 1925.

Rheims, Maurice. *L'Art 1900.* Paris, 1965.

Verne, Henri, and René Charance. *L'Art Décoratif Moderne en France.* Paris: Chez Hachette, 1925.

Vever, Henri: *La Bijouterie au XIX^me Siècle.* Vol. III. Paris: H. Floury, 1908.

Williams, W. C. *Motoring Mascots of the World.* Wisconsin, Motorbooks International, 1976.

## Articles in Periodicals and Journals

### ART ET DECORATION

Marx, Roger. "Les Maîtres Décorateurs Français: René Lalique," June 1899, pp. 13–22.

Beaunier, André. "Les Bijous de Lalique au Salon," August 1902, pp. 33–38.

Déstève, Tristan. "La Maison de René Lalique," November 1902, pp. 161–66.

Geoffroy, Gustave. "Des Bijoux; à propos de M. René Lalique," December 1905, pp. 177–88.

Anon. "René Lalique," July 1907, p. 20

Kahn, Gustave. "Lalique Verrier," September 1912, pp. 149–58.

Anon. "Des Bijoux Nouveau," May 1923, p. 151.

### MOBILIER ET DECORATION

Anon. "Les Verreries de René Lalique," September 1925, p. 32.

Anon. "René Lalique," January 1927.

Clouzot, Henri. "Daum, Verrerie d'Art," December 1930.

Anon. "Les Verreries de René Lalique," December 1932, pp. 213–19.

Anon. "L'Exposition de l'Oeuvre de René Lalique au Pavilion de Marsan," March 1933, pp. 95–102.

### L'ART DECORATIF

Bouyer, Raymond. "La Renaissance des Arts Décoratifs et sa Initiateur en France," July 1902, pp. 196–204.

Bayle, Paul. "Chez Lalique," May 1905, pp. 217–24.

Felice, Roger de. "Les Arts Appliqués au Salon d'Automne," September 1905, pp. 209–19.

Karageorgevitch, Prince Bojidar. "Les Objects d'Art au Salon des Artistes Françaises," No. 16, 1906, pp. 11–22.

### L'ART ET LES ARTISTES

Kahn, Gustave. "L'Art de René Lalique," Spring 1905, pp. 223–26.

———. "Les Verreries de René Lalique," Winter 1921, pp. 101–106.

Armand-Dayot, Madelaine. "Le Maître Verrier René Lalique," No. 26, 1933, pp. 273–77.

### LA RENAISSANCE DE L'ART ET DES INDUSTRIES DE LUXE

Anon. "La Parfumerie aux Arts Décoratifs," July 1925.

Gauthier, Maximilian. "Le Maître Verrier René Lalique à l'Exposition," September 1925, pp. 414–19.

Clouzot, Henri. "Le Flaconnage Artistique Moderne," January 1919, pp. 28–32.

Anon. "La Presse à L'Exposition des Oeuvres de René Lalique au Pavilion de Marsan," February/March 1933.

THE STUDIO

Anon. "The Lalique Exhibition (at Agnew's)," August 1905, pp. 127–34.

Anon. "Lalique Glass," June 1919, pp. 126–27.

Last, D. W. "Car Figureheads: The Development by René Lalique of a Modern Field for Illuminated Glass," February 1931, pp. 129–30.

CONNOISSEUR

Gomes-Ferreira, Maria Theresa. "René Lalique at the Calouste Gulbenkian Museum, Lisbon," 1971, pp. 241–49.

McClinton, Katharine Morrison. "René Lalique: Sculptor," October 1980, pp. 119–26.

Dawes, Nicholas M. "Lalique Alert," March 1984, pp. 20–21.

MISCELLANEOUS PERIODICALS

Tisserand, Ernest. "L'Art de René Lalique," L'Illustration, November 1932, pp. 223–26.

Courville, Paul. "L'Industrie du Verre en France," L'Européen, June 1, 1934.

Haraucourt, Edmond. "A Salon of French Taste," Arts and Decoration, December 1921, pp. 91–94.

———. "René Lalique et la Verrerie d'Alsace," Revue de l'Alsace Française, August 18, 1923.

Mourey, Gabriel. "Lalique's Glassware," Commercial Art, July 1926, pp. 32–37.

Cresswell, Howell S. "Modern Glass," Good Furniture and Decoration, September 1929, pp. 160–61.

Hayot, Monelle. "L'Atelier de René Lalique," L'Oeuil, March 1977, pp. 22–29.

Demoriane, Helene. "Verres signé Lalique," Connaissance des Arts, April 1970, pp. 112–17.

Anon. "A New and Great Craftsman in France," The Craftsman, October 1912, p. 75.

Stables, Mrs. Gordon. "Lalique," Artwork, May 1927, p. 33.

Anon. "Sand into Glass," Fortune, May 1930.

Mundhenk, B. L. "Lalique and Lalique-type Glass Ornaments," The Classic Car, Winter 1963, pp. 27–31.

Clendinin, Dorothy. "The Hood Ornaments of Lalique," Road and Track, June 1974, pp. 50–52.

Ashelford, Jane. "Lalique's Glass Church," Journal of the Decorative Arts Society (U.K.), No. 4, 1980, p. 28.

Anon. "An Interview with Marie-Claude Lalique," Collector Editions, Summer 1983, p. 25.

# Index

Note: page numbers in *italics* refer to illustrations or their captions